Copyright © 2023 by Daniel W. Marshall (Author)

All rights reserved. This book or any portion thereof may not be reproduced or used in any manner whatsoever without the express written permission of the publisher except for the use of brief quotations in a book review.

This book is copyright protected. This is only for personal use. You cannot amend, distributor, sell, use, quote or paraphrase any part or the content within this book without the consent of the author. Please note the information contained within this document is for educational and entertainment purposes only. Every attempt has been made to provide accurate, up to date and reliable complete information. No warranties of any kind are expressed or implied.

Readers acknowledge that the author is not engaging in the rendering of legal, financial, medical or professional advice. The content of this book has been derived from various sources. Please consult a licensed professional before attempting any techniques outlined in this book.

By reading this document, the readers agree that under no circumstances are the author responsible for any losses, direct or indirect, which are incurred as a result of the use of information contained within this document, including but not limited to errors, omissions or inaccuracies.

Thank you very much for reading this book.

Title: DAO: Empowering Communities with ICP-Powered Decentralization

Subtitle: A Comprehensive Guide to Implementing, Managing, and Thriving in the Decentralized World

Author: Daniel W. Marshall

Table of Contents

Introduction 6
The Dawn of Decentralized Governance: Unveiling the Internet Computer DAO System 6
The Essence of ICP DAO System: A Paradigm Shift in Governance 10
Network Nervous System (NNS): The Pulse of ICP Governance 16

Chapter 1: The Technological Foundation of ICP DAOs 23
Canister Smart Contracts: Building Blocks of Decentralized Applications 23
Chain-key Cryptography: Securing the Foundations of ICP DAO System 31
Asynchronous Byzantine Fault Tolerance (aBFT): Ensuring Network Resilience 38
Subnets: Fostering Diversity and Scalability in the ICP DAO Ecosystem 45

Chapter 2: The Mechanics of ICP DAOs 53
Proposal Creation and Voting Process: Empowering Community Participation 53
Governance Tokenomics: Aligning Incentives and Empowering DAOs 60
DAO Evolution and Adaptation: Embracing the Dynamic Landscape 67
Securing ICP DAOs: Protecting Assets and Maintaining Trust 74

Chapter 3: ICP DAOs in Action: Empowering Real-World Applications 81
Community-Driven Governance: ICP DAOs in the Realm of Non-Profit Organizations 81
Decentralized Finance (DeFi) and ICP DAOs: Redefining Financial Services 88
Social Impact and Community Initiatives: ICP DAOs for the Greater Good 95
Unlocking Creativity and Innovation: ICP DAOs in the Arts and Entertainment 103

Chapter 4: The Future of ICP DAOs: A Vision for Decentralized Governance 110
Evolving Governance Models: ICP DAOs as a Paradigm for Modern Governance 110
Scalability and Sustainability: Addressing the Challenges of Growth 116
Interoperability and Ecosystem Integration: Connecting ICP DAOs to the Wider Blockchain Landscape 123
Empowering Individuals and Communities: ICP DAOs as a Tool for Inclusive Governance 129

Chapter 5: Legal and Regulatory Considerations for ICP DAOs 136
Navigating the Legal Landscape: Understanding the Regulatory Framework for ICP DAOs 136
Intellectual Property Rights (IPR) and ICP DAOs: Protecting Innovation in the Digital Age 143
Taxation and Financial Compliance: Navigating Tax Implications for ICP DAOs 150

Data Privacy and Security: Protecting User Data in the ICP DAO Ecosystem *157*

Chapter 6: Realizing the Potential of ICP DAOs: A Practical Guide for Implementation **165**

Designing and Implementing an ICP DAO: A Step-by-Step Approach *165*

Community Engagement and Stakeholder Participation Strategies *172*

Managing Risk and Mitigating Challenges in ICP DAOs. 180

Measuring Success and Assessing Impact: Evaluating the Performance of ICP DAOs *188*

Conclusion **195**

Recapping the Transformative Potential of ICP DAOs – A Paradigm Shift in Governance *195*

Addressing Future Challenges and Opportunities - Paving the Way for Widespread Adoption *205*

A Call to Action: Embracing the Future of Decentralized Governance with ICP DAOs *216*

Glossary **230**

Potential References **235**

Introduction

The Dawn of Decentralized Governance: Unveiling the Internet Computer DAO System

In the dynamic landscape of decentralized technologies, a revolutionary force is reshaping the future of governance — the Internet Computer DAO system. As the world witnesses an increasing interest in decentralized autonomous organizations (DAOs), the emergence of the Internet Computer Protocol (ICP) as a cornerstone for decentralized governance signifies a paradigm shift in how communities collaborate, make decisions, and drive innovation. This chapter unveils the dawn of decentralized governance, focusing on the transformative capabilities of the ICP DAO system.

Unveiling the Internet Computer DAO System

At the heart of this groundbreaking transformation is the Internet Computer Protocol (ICP), a blockchain project that redefines the possibilities of decentralized computation. The ICP DAO system is not just a technological innovation; it represents a fundamental reimagining of how individuals, organizations, and communities can govern themselves in a digital era.

Decoding the Core Principles: The ICP DAO system is built upon a set of core principles that set it apart from traditional governance structures. At its essence, the system aims to foster transparency, inclusivity, and resilience. Unlike centralized models where power tends to concentrate in the hands of a few, the ICP DAO system is designed to distribute decision-making authority, ensuring that no single entity holds undue influence.

The Role of Smart Contracts: Central to the functionality of the ICP DAO system are smart contracts deployed within canisters, which serve as the building blocks of decentralized applications (DApps). These smart contracts operate on the principle of code as law, executing predefined rules without the need for intermediaries. This not only streamlines processes but also enhances the security and trustworthiness of the entire governance framework.

Introducing the Network Nervous System (NNS): At the core of ICP's governance mechanism is the Network Nervous System (NNS), a decentralized decision-making entity that plays a pivotal role in the evolution of the protocol. The NNS is not just a governance tool; it's the pulse of the entire ICP ecosystem. It enables token holders to propose and vote on changes, upgrades, and improvements, making the system adaptable to the evolving needs of its user base.

The Decentralization Imperative: Decentralization is more than a buzzword in the context of ICP DAOs; it's a fundamental requirement. The system leverages a robust consensus mechanism known as Asynchronous Byzantine Fault Tolerance (aBFT) to ensure the resilience of the network. This cryptographic approach mitigates the risks associated with malicious actors and ensures the continued operation of the ICP DAOs even in adverse conditions.

Subnets: Fostering Diversity and Scalability: In the ever-expanding digital landscape, diversity and scalability are crucial components of a robust decentralized ecosystem. ICP DAOs leverage subnets — independent blockchains within the larger network — to achieve both. These subnets enhance the system's adaptability, enabling it to accommodate a wide range of applications and use cases.

As we embark on this exploration of the Internet Computer DAO system, the following chapters will delve into the technological foundations, mechanics, real-world applications, and the future trajectory of ICP DAOs. Each facet of this journey contributes to our understanding of how decentralized governance, powered by the Internet Computer Protocol, is poised to reshape the fabric of our digital society. Join us as we unravel the intricacies of ICP DAOs and witness the unfolding of a new era in governance

— a future where power is distributed, decisions are collective, and innovation knows no bounds.

The Essence of ICP DAO System: A Paradigm Shift in Governance

In the vast landscape of blockchain and decentralized technologies, the Internet Computer Protocol (ICP) DAO system emerges as a beacon of innovation, promising not only to redefine governance but to usher in a paradigm shift in the way societies organize and make decisions. As we embark on this exploration of the essence of the ICP DAO system, we delve deep into the core principles that underpin its design and its potential to transform traditional governance structures.

The Core Principles of ICP DAO System

Transparency as a Foundation: At the heart of the ICP DAO system lies a commitment to transparency. Unlike traditional governance models where decision-making processes are often opaque and centralized, ICP DAOs operate on a principle of openness. The underlying blockchain technology, with its immutability and transparency features, ensures that every decision, transaction, and modification is recorded and accessible to all participants. This transparency not only fosters trust but also empowers individuals within the community by providing them with a clear view of the decision-making process.

Inclusivity in Decision-Making: One of the defining features of the ICP DAO system is its inclusivity. Traditional governance structures often suffer from exclusivity, where a select few hold decision-making power. In contrast, ICP DAOs empower a broad spectrum of participants by allowing them to engage in the decision-making process. Through mechanisms like token-based voting, stakeholders, regardless of their status or background, have a say in shaping the direction of the DAO. This inclusive approach not only democratizes governance but also ensures a diversity of perspectives, contributing to more robust and well-informed decisions.

Code as Law: Central to the functioning of the ICP DAO system is the concept of "code as law." Smart contracts, deployed within canisters, embody the rules and regulations that govern the DAO. These contracts are executed automatically, eliminating the need for intermediaries or centralized authorities to enforce compliance. This not only streamlines processes but also reduces the potential for human error or bias in decision-making. The reliance on code as the governing force ensures that rules are applied consistently and transparently, fostering a system built on integrity and predictability.

Decentralization as a Pillar: Decentralization is not just a feature of the ICP DAO system; it's a foundational pillar. The distributed nature of the network, powered by the Network Nervous System (NNS), ensures that decision-making authority is not concentrated in a single entity. This decentralization mitigates the risk of a single point of failure and enhances the system's resilience against external threats. The Asynchronous Byzantine Fault Tolerance (aBFT) consensus mechanism further strengthens the network, making it robust and resistant to malicious attacks.

Empowering Through Governance Tokenomics: Governance tokenomics is a key element in the ICP DAO system, aligning incentives and empowering participants. By holding governance tokens, individuals gain the right to propose and vote on changes within the DAO. This economic model ensures that those with a vested interest in the success of the system have a direct influence on its governance. The alignment of incentives through tokenomics creates a self-sustaining ecosystem where participants are motivated to contribute to the growth and stability of the DAO.

ICP DAO System in Practice

Adaptability and Evolution: The essence of the ICP DAO system lies not only in its design principles but also in its adaptability to a dynamic landscape. DAOs powered by

ICP are not static entities; they evolve and adapt to the changing needs and challenges of their communities. The DAO evolution process, facilitated by the NNS, allows for upgrades, improvements, and modifications based on the consensus of the community. This inherent adaptability positions ICP DAOs as living organisms capable of responding to the ever-shifting terrain of decentralized governance.

Securing ICP DAOs: The essence of the ICP DAO system extends to its commitment to security. As decentralized networks become targets for malicious actors, ICP DAOs leverage advanced cryptographic techniques and consensus mechanisms to secure their operations. The combination of chain-key cryptography and aBFT not only ensures the integrity of transactions but also fortifies the network against potential vulnerabilities. In a landscape where security is paramount, ICP DAOs stand as bastions of resilience.

The Transformative Impact of ICP DAOs

Redesigning Power Dynamics: At its core, the ICP DAO system challenges traditional power dynamics by redistributing authority and decision-making. The shift from centralized control to decentralized governance signifies a broader societal change where individuals are no longer mere subjects of decisions but active participants in shaping the rules that govern them. This redefinition of power dynamics has far-reaching implications, transcending the realm of blockchain and influencing how societies conceptualize authority and agency.

Beyond Governance: Social and Economic Implications: The essence of the ICP DAO system extends beyond its immediate governance implications to touch upon broader social and economic dimensions. By fostering transparency, inclusivity, and decentralization, ICP DAOs have the potential to address systemic issues present in traditional models. The economic implications of governance tokenomics, for instance, redefine how value is distributed within a community, creating a more equitable system where contributors are appropriately rewarded for their participation.

Unlocking Innovation and Collaboration: ICP DAOs act as catalysts for innovation and collaboration by providing a platform where diverse stakeholders can converge. The decentralized nature of decision-making fosters an environment where ideas can flourish without the constraints of traditional bureaucratic processes. Whether in the realms of art, finance, or social impact, the essence of ICP DAOs lies in their ability to unlock creativity and innovation, allowing communities to harness their collective intelligence for the greater good.

In the following chapters, we will delve into the technological foundations, mechanics, real-world applications, legal considerations, and the practical implementation of ICP DAOs. Each facet contributes to the overarching narrative of a paradigm shift in governance — a narrative where the essence of the ICP DAO system reshapes how societies organize, collaborate, and thrive in the decentralized landscape. Join us on this journey as we unravel the transformative potential of ICP DAOs and explore the intricate web of possibilities they weave for the future of decentralized governance.

Network Nervous System (NNS): The Pulse of ICP Governance

In the intricate tapestry of decentralized governance powered by the Internet Computer Protocol (ICP), a pulsating heartbeat resonates, guiding the rhythm of decision-making and evolution. This vital force is none other than the Network Nervous System (NNS), an ingenious mechanism that serves as the pulsating core of ICP governance. This chapter unravels the significance, functionality, and transformative power of the NNS, illustrating how it shapes the very essence of decentralized decision-making within the ICP DAO system.

Understanding the Network Nervous System

Conceptual Foundations: At its conceptual core, the Network Nervous System (NNS) embodies the decentralized intelligence that governs the Internet Computer Protocol. Drawing inspiration from the human nervous system, the NNS operates as a distributed decision-making entity, orchestrating the intricate dance of proposals, voting, and execution within the ICP ecosystem. It is not merely a governance tool but a dynamic force that ensures the adaptability and resilience of the entire network.

Decentralized Decision-Making: The NNS stands as the linchpin of ICP governance, enabling decentralized decision-making on a scale never seen before. Unlike traditional systems where decisions are concentrated in the hands of a select few, the NNS empowers a diverse community of token holders to actively participate in shaping the future of the protocol. Through a consensus-driven process, stakeholders can propose, discuss, and vote on changes, upgrades, and modifications, fostering a truly democratic approach to governance.

Token-based Participation: Central to the NNS's functionality is the concept of token-based participation. Participants in the ICP ecosystem hold governance tokens, granting them the right to partake in decision-making processes. The number of tokens one possesses directly correlates with the influence they wield in the governance of the network. This token-based model aligns the interests of stakeholders with the success and stability of the ICP DAO system, creating a self-sustaining and incentive-driven ecosystem.

Proposal Lifecycle: The NNS orchestrates a meticulously designed proposal lifecycle that encapsulates the journey of an idea from inception to execution. Any participant in the ICP ecosystem can initiate a proposal, presenting their vision for changes or enhancements to the network. These proposals undergo a thorough review process, allowing the community to engage in discussions, provide feedback, and collectively refine the propositions. The final stage involves a democratic vote where token holders cast their votes, determining the fate of the proposal. Successful proposals are then implemented through smart contracts, ensuring a seamless and transparent transition from idea to action.

The Pulse of ICP Governance: Real-time Adaptability

Dynamic Evolution: The Network Nervous System breathes life into the concept of dynamic evolution within the ICP DAO system. The ability to adapt to changing circumstances and requirements is not a mere feature; it is a defining characteristic. The NNS enables the protocol to evolve, incorporating improvements and innovations proposed by the community. This dynamic evolution ensures that the ICP DAO system remains at the forefront of technological advancements, responding swiftly to challenges and opportunities in the decentralized landscape.

Continuous Improvement: At its essence, the NNS embodies the spirit of continuous improvement. The decentralized nature of decision-making ensures that no single entity or authority can stifle progress. Instead, the NNS acts as a facilitator for continuous refinement, driving the ICP ecosystem towards optimal performance. Through a cyclical process of proposal, discussion, voting, and implementation, the NNS fosters a culture of perpetual enhancement, reflecting the organic and iterative nature of decentralized governance.

Decentralized Software Updates: A notable manifestation of the NNS's pulse is its role in facilitating decentralized software updates. Unlike centralized systems where updates are dictated by a central authority, the NNS empowers the community to collectively decide on the implementation of software changes. This decentralized approach not only enhances security by mitigating the risk of single points of failure but also ensures that software updates align with the diverse needs and preferences of the ICP community.

Security and Resilience: The Protective Shield of NNS

Mitigating Threats through Decentralization: Security is paramount in the decentralized landscape, and the NNS serves as a formidable shield against potential threats. By distributing decision-making authority across a diverse network of participants, the NNS mitigates the risk of malicious attacks or attempts to compromise the integrity of the ICP DAO system. The decentralized consensus mechanisms, coupled with the Asynchronous Byzantine

Fault Tolerance (aBFT) protocol, fortify the network, making it robust and resistant to external threats.

Self-Healing Capabilities: In the event of unforeseen challenges or disruptions, the NNS exhibits self-healing capabilities. The decentralized nature of the network ensures that, even in the face of adversity, the ICP DAO system can adapt and recover. The NNS acts as a safeguard, autonomously responding to issues and guiding the network towards stability. This inherent resilience is a testament to the decentralized design principles that underpin the ICP DAO system.

Challenges and Evolution of the Network Nervous System

Scalability Considerations: While the NNS stands as a paragon of decentralized governance, it is not without challenges. Scalability is a consideration as the ICP ecosystem continues to grow. The NNS must evolve to handle an expanding network, ensuring that decision-making processes remain efficient and inclusive. Proposals for scalability enhancements, driven by the NNS itself, showcase the system's commitment to addressing challenges proactively.

Interoperability and Integration: As decentralized technologies evolve, the NNS grapples with the imperative of interoperability and ecosystem integration. The ability of the ICP DAO system to seamlessly interact with other blockchain networks and decentralized applications (DApps) is crucial for its long-term success. The NNS, as the pulse of ICP governance, plays a pivotal role in shaping strategies for interoperability, fostering collaboration with the broader blockchain landscape.

The NNS in Action: Realizing the Vision of ICP DAOs

Community-Driven Innovation: The NNS, as the pulse of ICP governance, propels community-driven innovation. Through its decentralized decision-making processes, the ICP ecosystem becomes a fertile ground for diverse ideas to flourish. Community members, irrespective of their backgrounds or affiliations, actively contribute to the evolution of the protocol. This community-driven approach not only democratizes innovation but also ensures that the ICP DAO system remains a reflection of the collective intelligence of its stakeholders.

Evolving Governance Models: The NNS catalyzes the evolution of governance models within the ICP ecosystem. The decentralized decision-making processes facilitated by the NNS provide a blueprint for modern governance. As traditional structures grapple with inefficiencies and centralization, ICP DAOs, guided by the NNS, showcase a path towards governance that is adaptive, inclusive, and resilient. The evolving governance models redefine how organizations and communities collaborate, inspiring a paradigm shift in the broader landscape of governance.

Conclusion: The Rhythmic Future of ICP DAOs

As we conclude our exploration of the Network Nervous System, the heartbeat of ICP governance, we recognize its transformative impact on the decentralized landscape. The NNS, with its decentralized decision-making, dynamic evolution, and security features, emerges as more than a governance tool; it symbolizes the heartbeat of a future where power is distributed, innovation is boundless, and governance is truly inclusive. Join us in the ensuing chapters as we delve deeper into the technological foundations, mechanics, real-world applications, legal considerations, and the practical implementation of ICP DAOs. The NNS sets the rhythmic pulse for a decentralized future, and our journey into the heart of ICP DAOs is just beginning.

Chapter 1: The Technological Foundation of ICP DAOs

Canister Smart Contracts: Building Blocks of Decentralized Applications

In the ever-expanding realm of decentralized technologies, the building blocks of innovation lie in the hands of smart contracts. Within the Internet Computer Protocol (ICP) DAO system, these intelligent, self-executing contracts find a home within entities known as canisters. This section unveils the intricate workings of canister smart contracts, exploring how they serve as the bedrock upon which decentralized applications (DApps) are constructed, and how they contribute to the robust technological foundation of ICP DAOs.

The Genesis of Canister Smart Contracts

Understanding Smart Contracts: At the heart of decentralized systems, smart contracts embody the promise of trustless and automated execution of predefined agreements. In their simplest form, smart contracts are self-executing pieces of code that run on a blockchain. They encode the rules and terms of an agreement, ensuring that once conditions are met, the contract automatically enforces and executes the specified actions without the need for intermediaries. This characteristic aligns perfectly with the principles of decentralization and transparency that underpin the ICP DAO system.

Canisters as Intelligent Containers: In the context of the ICP ecosystem, smart contracts are encapsulated within entities known as canisters. Think of canisters as intelligent containers or units of computation that hold the code and state of a smart contract. These canisters are not merely storage units but dynamic entities capable of executing code, maintaining state, and communicating with other canisters within the decentralized network. They form the foundational infrastructure upon which the entire ICP DAO system operates.

Architectural Framework of Canisters

Secure and Decentralized Computation: Canisters operate within a secure and decentralized computational environment, ensuring that the principles of trust and transparency are woven into the very fabric of ICP DAOs. The architecture of canisters leverages the underlying blockchain to provide a secure execution environment. This not only enhances the reliability of the smart contracts but also mitigates the risk of malicious attacks, a crucial consideration in the landscape of decentralized applications.

Inter-Canister Communication: An innovative feature of canisters is their ability to communicate with each other seamlessly. This inter-canister communication is a cornerstone of the ICP DAO system's functionality. Canisters can exchange messages and data, enabling the development of complex, interconnected decentralized applications. This capability fosters a modular and scalable approach to building applications within the ICP ecosystem, allowing for a diverse range of use cases and functionalities.

Decentralized Applications (DApps): The Output of Canister Smart Contracts

Canisters and DApp Development: Canister smart contracts serve as the backbone of decentralized applications, empowering developers to create a new generation of software that operates on principles of decentralization, transparency, and immutability. Decentralized applications, or DApps, are not confined to the limitations of traditional, centrally controlled software. Instead, they leverage the power of canisters to execute code in a trustless manner, providing users with a level of security and autonomy that was previously elusive.

Immutable Code and Transparent Execution: The immutability of smart contracts within canisters ensures that the code governing DApps remains tamper-proof once deployed. This immutability is a key feature of canister smart contracts, aligning with the broader ethos of blockchain technology. Users can trust that the rules encoded within a smart contract will be executed exactly as intended, without the risk of interference or alteration. The transparent execution of code adds an additional layer of trust, allowing users to verify the operations of a DApp in real-time.

Chain-key Cryptography: Securing the Foundations of ICP DAO System

Asynchronous Byzantine Fault Tolerance (aBFT): Ensuring Network Resilience

Subnets: Fostering Diversity and Scalability in the ICP DAO Ecosystem

Integration of Tokens and Governance: A pivotal aspect of canister smart contracts within the ICP DAO system is their integration with governance tokens. These tokens play a dual role, serving as both a medium of exchange within the decentralized ecosystem and a mechanism for participating in the governance of the network. Canister smart contracts facilitate the seamless integration of governance tokens, enabling token holders to actively engage in the decision-making processes of the ICP DAO system.

The Life Cycle of Canister Smart Contracts

Deployment and Initialization: The journey of a canister smart contract begins with deployment. Developers initiate the deployment process, specifying the code and initial state of the smart contract. Once deployed, the canister becomes an active entity within the ICP ecosystem, ready to execute its predefined functions. Initialization involves setting up the initial conditions and parameters that govern the behavior of the smart contract.

Execution and Interactions: Canister smart contracts are dynamic entities that execute code in response to external triggers or messages. Interactions can come from users, other canisters, or even external systems. This ability to interact with the broader ICP DAO system and beyond makes canisters versatile and integral to the interconnected nature of decentralized applications.

Upgradeability and Evolution: One of the distinguishing features of canisters is their upgradeability. As the ICP DAO system evolves, smart contracts can be upgraded to incorporate new features, fix bugs, or adapt to changing requirements. This upgradability ensures that the ICP ecosystem remains at the forefront of technological advancements, providing a flexible and future-proof foundation for decentralized governance.

Security Considerations in Canister Smart Contracts

Chain-key Cryptography: Securing the foundations of ICP DAOs involves robust cryptographic mechanisms, and canisters leverage chain-key cryptography as part of their security architecture. Chain-key cryptography ensures that the chain of blocks forming the ICP blockchain remains secure and resistant to tampering. It involves the use of cryptographic keys to sign and verify blocks, providing a secure and verifiable ledger of transactions.

Ensuring Network Resilience through Asynchronous Byzantine Fault Tolerance (aBFT)

Fault Tolerance in Decentralized Networks: In the decentralized landscape, where nodes operate independently, ensuring network resilience is paramount. Asynchronous Byzantine Fault Tolerance (aBFT) is a consensus mechanism employed by ICP DAOs to achieve fault tolerance. In simple terms, aBFT ensures that the network can reach consensus and continue to operate even in the presence of faulty or malicious nodes. This resilience is crucial for maintaining the integrity and functionality of canister smart contracts.

Fostering Diversity and Scalability in the ICP DAO Ecosystem through Subnets

The Concept of Subnets: Subnets represent a fundamental architectural element within the ICP DAO ecosystem, contributing to both diversity and scalability. A subnet is essentially an independent blockchain within the larger ICP network. It operates with its own set of rules and governance, fostering diversity by allowing different subnets to cater to specific use cases, industries, or communities. This modular approach enhances the overall scalability of the ICP DAO system.

Enhancing Scalability: Scalability is a critical consideration in the design of decentralized systems, especially as user numbers and transaction volumes increase. Subnets play a key role in enhancing scalability by distributing the computational load across multiple independent blockchains. This approach ensures that the ICP DAO system can handle a growing number of transactions and applications without compromising performance or decentralization.

Conclusion: Canister Smart Contracts as the Pillars of ICP DAOs

As we delve into the technological foundation of ICP DAOs, the role of canister smart contracts emerges as pivotal. These intelligent containers of code not only serve as the building blocks of decentralized applications but also encapsulate the principles of trustless execution, security, and upgradeability. Canisters, operating within a secure and decentralized computational environment, interact seamlessly with governance tokens, contributing to the dynamic and interconnected nature of the ICP DAO system. In the subsequent chapters, we will explore the mechanics of ICP DAOs, governance tokenomics, and the evolution of decentralized decision-making. The journey through the technological foundations sets the stage for understanding how canister smart contracts, in synergy with other elements, shape the decentralized future envisioned by the Internet Computer Protocol.

Chain-key Cryptography: Securing the Foundations of ICP DAO System

In the landscape of decentralized technologies, security is paramount, and at the core of the Internet Computer Protocol (ICP) DAO system's security architecture lies the robust mechanism of chain-key cryptography. This section delves into the intricacies of chain-key cryptography, unveiling its role in securing the foundations of ICP DAOs and ensuring the integrity and immutability of the decentralized network.

Understanding Chain-key Cryptography

Cryptographic Foundations: Chain-key cryptography is a cornerstone of the security framework underpinning the ICP DAO system. At its essence, cryptography involves the use of mathematical techniques to secure communication, protect information, and verify the authenticity of transactions. In the context of blockchain and decentralized systems, cryptographic mechanisms ensure that data remains confidential, transactions are secure, and the integrity of the entire network is preserved.

The Blockchain Ledger: At the heart of ICP DAOs is the blockchain, a distributed and immutable ledger that records transactions in a secure and transparent manner. Chain-key cryptography is instrumental in securing this ledger, ensuring that each block in the chain is cryptographically linked to the previous one, forming an unbroken and tamper-resistant sequence of transactions. This cryptographic linking, achieved through the use of hash functions and digital signatures, creates the backbone of the decentralized network's security.

Chain-keys and Their Role in ICP DAO Security

Defining Chain-keys: In the context of ICP DAOs, chain-keys play a pivotal role in securing the blockchain. A chain-key is a cryptographic key associated with a specific chain of blocks. It serves as the mechanism by which nodes in the network validate the authenticity and integrity of transactions. Each block is signed with the chain-key of the previous block, creating a continuous and verifiable sequence. This cryptographic linkage ensures that any attempt to alter a block would require changing all subsequent blocks, an impractical and computationally infeasible task.

The Immutability Guarantee: Chain-key cryptography contributes significantly to the immutability of the blockchain, a fundamental characteristic of decentralized systems. Once a block is added to the chain and signed with the chain-key, it becomes part of an unalterable history. This immutability is crucial for establishing trust within the ICP

DAO system. Participants can be confident that the recorded transactions are secure, unchangeable, and reflect an accurate representation of the history of the network.

Ensuring Network Resilience through Asynchronous Byzantine Fault Tolerance (aBFT)

Subnets: Fostering Diversity and Scalability in the ICP DAO Ecosystem

Security in a Decentralized Environment: Decentralization introduces unique security challenges, and chain-key cryptography is designed to address these challenges effectively. In a decentralized network, nodes operate independently, and the consensus on the state of the blockchain must be achieved in the presence of potential adversarial nodes. Chain-key cryptography, combined with consensus mechanisms such as Asynchronous Byzantine Fault Tolerance (aBFT), ensures that the network remains resilient and secure even in the face of malicious actors.

Decentralized Consensus and Chain-keys

Consensus Mechanisms: In the decentralized world of ICP DAOs, achieving consensus—agreement among nodes on the state of the blockchain—is a critical aspect of security. Consensus mechanisms like aBFT ensure that even if some nodes behave maliciously or experience faults, the network can still agree on the validity of transactions. Chain-keys play a crucial role in this consensus process by providing a cryptographic basis for verifying the integrity of the blocks proposed by nodes. Each node can independently verify that a proposed block is signed with the correct chain-key, ensuring that the proposed transaction history is valid.

Immutable Verification: The use of chain-keys in the consensus process provides an immutable verification mechanism. As nodes reach consensus on the next block in the chain, they are essentially agreeing on the chain-key associated with that block. This agreement is achieved through cryptographic verification, and once consensus is reached, the block becomes part of the immutable history of the blockchain. This cryptographic agreement, facilitated by chain-key cryptography, is essential for maintaining the trustworthiness and security of the ICP DAO system.

Enhancing Security Through Transparency and Verifiability

Transparent Execution: Transparency is a key principle in decentralized systems, and chain-key cryptography contributes to the transparent execution of transactions within ICP DAOs. Every participant in the network has access to the entire history of transactions, and the cryptographic linkage between blocks ensures that any attempt to modify historical transactions would be immediately evident. This transparency not only builds trust among participants but also allows for independent verification of the correctness and security of the ICP DAO system.

Verifiability and Trustlessness: Chain-key cryptography enhances the trustlessness of the ICP DAO system by providing a verifiable mechanism for participants to validate the state of the blockchain. Participants can independently verify the integrity of each block by checking its cryptographic signature with the associated chain-key. This verifiability ensures that participants do not need to trust a central authority; instead, they can trust the cryptographic principles that govern the decentralized network. Trustlessness, a fundamental tenet of decentralized systems, is reinforced through the cryptographic foundations laid by chain-key cryptography.

The Role of Chain-key Cryptography in Governance Tokenomics

Token-based Governance: Governance within the ICP DAO system is intricately tied to the use of governance tokens, and chain-key cryptography plays a role in securing the mechanisms through which these tokens are utilized. Governance tokens represent a participant's stake and influence within the network, and their secure operation relies on cryptographic principles. Chain-keys are employed to sign transactions involving governance tokens, ensuring the security and integrity of token-based governance processes.

Looking Ahead: Challenges and Evolutions in Chain-key Cryptography

Scalability Challenges: While chain-key cryptography has proven effective in securing the foundations of ICP DAOs, challenges related to scalability must be addressed as the network grows. As the number of transactions and participants increases, the computational load associated with cryptographic operations may become a bottleneck. Research and development efforts are ongoing to optimize and scale chain-key cryptography, ensuring that it continues to provide a secure foundation for the evolving needs of the ICP DAO system.

Interoperability and Future Considerations: The landscape of decentralized technologies is dynamic, and considerations of interoperability with other blockchain networks and evolving cryptographic standards must be factored into the future of chain-key cryptography. As ICP DAOs interact with a broader ecosystem, ensuring compatibility and security across diverse cryptographic frameworks becomes an important aspect of the ongoing development and maturation of the ICP protocol.

Conclusion: Chain-key Cryptography as the Guardian of Trust in ICP DAOs

In the intricate architecture of the Internet Computer Protocol DAO system, chain-key cryptography emerges as the guardian of trust and security. Its role in securing the blockchain, facilitating decentralized consensus, and providing the cryptographic foundations for governance tokenomics is pivotal. As we navigate through the technological foundations of ICP DAOs, the robustness of chain-key cryptography becomes evident, laying the groundwork for a decentralized future where participants can trust the integrity and transparency of the systems they engage with. In the subsequent chapters, we will explore further components of ICP DAOs, governance mechanisms, and the real-world applications that leverage this secure and decentralized foundation.

Asynchronous Byzantine Fault Tolerance (aBFT): Ensuring Network Resilience

In the intricate web of decentralized systems, resilience in the face of potential faults or malicious actors is a foundational pillar. Asynchronous Byzantine Fault Tolerance (aBFT) emerges as a sophisticated and robust consensus mechanism within the Internet Computer Protocol (ICP) DAO system, fortifying the network against adversarial conditions. This section unravels the significance of aBFT, exploring its role in ensuring network resilience, maintaining consensus, and upholding the integrity of ICP DAOs.

Understanding Byzantine Fault Tolerance

Challenges in Decentralized Consensus: Decentralized networks are inherently susceptible to challenges arising from node failures, communication delays, or malicious actors. Byzantine Fault Tolerance (BFT) is a class of consensus algorithms designed to address these challenges by ensuring that the network can reach consensus even when some nodes behave arbitrarily or maliciously. In the context of ICP DAOs, where decentralized decision-making is paramount, aBFT stands out as a powerful mechanism for achieving consensus among nodes in a Byzantine environment.

Byzantine Generals' Problem: The concept of Byzantine Fault Tolerance is rooted in the Byzantine Generals' Problem, a classic thought experiment in computer science. In this scenario, a group of generals, each commanding a segment of the Byzantine army, must coordinate their attack or retreat. Some generals may be traitors, sending conflicting messages to create confusion. The challenge is to devise a protocol that ensures loyal generals can reach a consensus on a common plan of action despite the potential presence of traitorous generals. The analogy extends to decentralized networks, where nodes must coordinate to agree on the state of the system, even in the presence of potentially malicious nodes.

aBFT: The Asynchronous Advancement

Traditional BFT Algorithms: Traditional Byzantine Fault Tolerance algorithms operate under synchronous assumptions, requiring nodes to have synchronized clocks and setting specific time bounds for message delays. While effective in certain scenarios, these synchronous BFT algorithms face challenges in the real-world, where network conditions can be unpredictable, and nodes may experience variable message delivery times. aBFT, or Asynchronous Byzantine Fault Tolerance, takes a significant leap forward by relaxing the synchronous assumptions, making it more adaptable to real-world decentralized environments.

The Mechanics of Asynchronous Byzantine Fault Tolerance

Consensus in an Asynchronous Environment: aBFT achieves consensus in an asynchronous environment, meaning that nodes in the network operate without the need for synchronized clocks or strict timing constraints. This asynchrony allows aBFT to be more resilient to unpredictable network conditions, communication delays, and potential adversarial behaviors. Nodes can independently propose blocks, communicate their proposals to others, and collectively agree on a consistent set of transactions without relying on precise timing assumptions.

Node Communication and Proposal Rounds: The mechanics of aBFT involve a series of proposal rounds, where nodes take turns proposing blocks to be added to the blockchain. In each round, a node proposes a block, and other nodes acknowledge or reject the proposal. The consensus is reached through a series of such rounds, with nodes converging on a common set of transactions to be included in the next block. Importantly, aBFT ensures that the consensus is achieved even if some nodes are faulty or malicious.

Ensuring Network Resilience: The Strength of aBFT

Mitigating Byzantine Failures: The primary strength of aBFT lies in its ability to mitigate Byzantine failures, where nodes in the network may behave arbitrarily or provide conflicting information. In a decentralized environment like ICP DAOs, where participants may have diverse interests, ensuring that the network can withstand malicious behaviors is crucial. aBFT achieves this by allowing honest nodes to reach consensus, even in the presence of a significant number of Byzantine or adversarial nodes.

Flexibility in Message Timing: The asynchronous nature of aBFT provides flexibility in message timing, allowing nodes to propose and acknowledge blocks without rigid time constraints. This flexibility is particularly valuable in decentralized networks where communication delays can vary widely. aBFT adapts to the dynamic and unpredictable nature of the network, ensuring that the consensus process remains resilient and efficient.

Decentralized Consensus in ICP DAOs: The aBFT Approach

The Role of aBFT in ICP DAO Consensus: In the context of ICP DAOs, decentralized consensus is a linchpin for effective and transparent decision-making. aBFT serves as the approach to achieving this consensus, allowing the network to agree on the state of the blockchain, the validity of transactions, and the execution of smart contracts. The resilience of aBFT ensures that the ICP DAO system can continue to operate even in the face of varying network conditions, node failures, or attempts at malicious manipulation.

Security and Immutability: The security and immutability of the ICP DAO blockchain are inherently tied to the consensus achieved through aBFT. By providing a mechanism for nodes to agree on the validity of transactions and the state of the system, aBFT contributes to the creation of a secure and tamper-resistant ledger. Once consensus is reached, the agreed-upon block becomes part of the blockchain's history, and the cryptographic linkage provided by chain-key cryptography further reinforces the immutability of the recorded transactions.

Challenges and Considerations in aBFT Implementation

Scalability Considerations: While aBFT offers significant advantages in terms of resilience and adaptability, scalability considerations must be addressed as the ICP DAO system grows. As the number of nodes and transactions increases, the computational and communication overhead associated with aBFT may become a limiting factor. Ongoing research and development aim to optimize aBFT implementations, ensuring that the consensus mechanism remains efficient and scalable in the face of network expansion.

Interoperability and Standardization: Interoperability with other blockchain networks and the establishment of standards for aBFT implementations are crucial considerations for the broader adoption of ICP DAOs. As decentralized ecosystems evolve, ensuring that aBFT-based consensus mechanisms can seamlessly interact with other protocols and networks becomes essential. Standardization efforts contribute to the creation of a cohesive and interoperable decentralized landscape.

Real-world Implications: aBFT in Action

Decentralized Governance: In the realm of ICP DAOs, aBFT becomes the backbone of decentralized governance. The consensus achieved through aBFT determines the rules, changes, and decisions that shape the trajectory of the decentralized network. Participants can trust that the governance processes are not susceptible to manipulation or arbitrary interference, as aBFT ensures that consensus is reached in a resilient and trustless manner.

Smart Contract Execution: aBFT plays a critical role in the execution of smart contracts within the ICP DAO system. Smart contracts, encapsulated within canisters and secured by chain-key cryptography, rely on aBFT to ensure that their execution is agreed upon by the network. The deterministic and secure nature of aBFT consensus provides participants with confidence in the outcomes of smart contract executions, contributing to the broader trustworthiness of the decentralized ecosystem.

Conclusion: The Resilient Foundation of ICP DAOs

Asynchronous Byzantine Fault Tolerance emerges as a cornerstone in the technological foundation of ICP DAOs, ensuring network resilience, security, and decentralized consensus. The aBFT approach, with its adaptability to asynchronous environments and mitigation of Byzantine failures, sets the stage for transparent and trustless decision-making within the ICP DAO system. In the following chapters, we will continue to unravel the intricacies of the ICP DAO architecture, exploring the role of subnets in fostering diversity and scalability and the integration of governance tokenomics in empowering decentralized governance. The journey into the decentralized future is guided by the resilience and adaptability encapsulated in the aBFT consensus mechanism.

Subnets: Fostering Diversity and Scalability in the ICP DAO Ecosystem

In the expansive landscape of decentralized technologies, the concept of subnets emerges as a pivotal architectural innovation within the Internet Computer Protocol (ICP) DAO system. Subnets represent more than just technical components; they embody a strategic approach to fostering diversity and scalability in the decentralized ecosystem. This section navigates through the intricacies of subnets, exploring how they contribute to the resilience, adaptability, and sustainable growth of ICP DAOs.

Understanding Subnets in Decentralized Systems

Architectural Diversity: At its core, a subnet is a distinct and independent blockchain within the broader ICP network. Unlike traditional blockchain architectures that operate as a single, monolithic entity, subnets introduce a modular and scalable approach to decentralized systems. Each subnet has its own set of rules, governance mechanisms, and consensus models, allowing for architectural diversity tailored to specific use cases, industries, or communities.

The Role of Subnets: Subnets play a multifaceted role within the ICP DAO ecosystem. They contribute to diversity by accommodating a range of decentralized applications

(DApps) with unique requirements. Simultaneously, subnets enhance scalability by distributing the computational load across multiple independent blockchains. This combination of diversity and scalability positions subnets as a fundamental building block for the growth and sustainability of ICP DAOs.

Enhancing Scalability through Subnets

Scalability Challenges in Decentralized Systems: Scalability is a perennial challenge in the world of decentralized systems, especially as user numbers and transaction volumes increase. Traditional blockchains often face limitations in processing speed and transaction throughput, leading to congestion and increased transaction costs during periods of high demand. Subnets address these scalability challenges by providing a framework for parallel processing and distributed computation.

Parallelization of Transactions: Within the ICP DAO ecosystem, subnets enable the parallelization of transactions. Instead of relying on a single blockchain to process all transactions, subnets allow for multiple blockchains to operate concurrently. This parallel processing capability enhances the overall throughput of the network, ensuring that ICP DAOs can handle a growing number of transactions without sacrificing performance or efficiency.

Fostering Diversity through Independent Subnets

Tailoring to Specific Use Cases: One of the key advantages of subnets is their ability to cater to specific use cases or industries. Different subnets can be tailored to meet the unique requirements of decentralized applications within particular domains. For example, a subnet optimized for decentralized finance (DeFi) may have governance rules and consensus mechanisms that align with the specific needs of financial applications, while another subnet focused on social impact initiatives may prioritize governance structures that align with non-profit organizations.

Custom Governance Mechanisms: Governance within a subnet is customizable, allowing for the implementation of governance mechanisms that best suit the needs and values of the participants in that particular subnet. This flexibility is a departure from the one-size-fits-all approach often seen in traditional centralized systems. Subnets empower communities to define their own governance models, fostering a sense of ownership and autonomy.

Interconnectivity: The Fabric of Subnet Collaboration

Interoperability Among Subnets: While subnets operate independently, they are not isolated entities within the ICP DAO ecosystem. Interconnectivity is a key feature that allows subnets to communicate with each other, enabling the exchange of information, assets, and functionalities. This inter-subnet communication is facilitated by the Network Nervous System (NNS), which serves as the overarching governance mechanism for the entire ICP network.

Cross-Subnet Collaboration: The ability for subnets to collaborate opens up a multitude of possibilities. For instance, a DApp developed on one subnet may leverage the services or functionalities provided by another subnet. This collaborative ecosystem encourages innovation, as developers and communities can benefit from the strengths of different subnets and create integrated solutions that transcend the limitations of any single subnet.

The Architecture of Subnets in ICP DAOs

Independent Blockchain Structure: Each subnet in the ICP DAO system operates as an independent blockchain with its own consensus mechanism, governance rules, and canister smart contracts. This independence ensures that the failure or malicious behavior of one subnet does not impact the overall functionality of the entire ICP network. The modular nature of subnets allows for upgrades, improvements, and adaptations specific to each subnet without requiring changes to the entire network.

Node Distribution and Diversity: Nodes within a subnet participate in the consensus mechanism and governance processes specific to that subnet. This distribution of nodes enhances the decentralization of the ICP DAO ecosystem. It ensures that decision-making power is distributed across multiple entities, reducing the risk of centralization and enhancing the network's resilience to attacks or failures.

Governance Tokenomics Across Subnets

Integration of Governance Tokens: Governance tokens, a fundamental component of decentralized systems, are integrated into the fabric of subnets within the ICP DAO ecosystem. These tokens serve as a mechanism for participants to influence decision-making processes within their respective subnets. The integration of governance tokens aligns with the broader principles of decentralized governance, where participants actively engage in shaping the rules and evolution of the network.

Token Utility Across Subnets: The utility of governance tokens extends beyond individual subnets. Participants holding governance tokens within one subnet may use them to participate in governance processes in other subnets, fostering a cross-subnet governance landscape. This interconnected tokenomics model ensures that participants have a stake in the governance of the entire ICP DAO system, promoting a holistic and collaborative approach to decentralized decision-making.

Challenges and Considerations in Subnet Design

Balancing Independence and Interoperability: The design of subnets involves a delicate balance between independence and interoperability. While independence allows subnets to cater to specific needs and use cases, interoperability ensures that the ICP DAO ecosystem remains cohesive and interconnected. Striking the right balance is crucial for creating a decentralized network that is both diverse and collaborative.

Security Across Subnets: Security considerations are paramount in the design and operation of subnets. Each subnet must implement robust security measures to protect against malicious attacks, ensuring the integrity of transactions and smart contracts within that subnet. Additionally, the inter-subnet communication must be secure to prevent vulnerabilities that could be exploited to compromise the overall ICP DAO system.

Real-world Applications: Subnets in Action

Industry-specific Subnets: The versatility of subnets becomes evident in their application to different industries. For example, an industry-specific subnet for healthcare may focus on ensuring the privacy and security of patient data, while a supply chain-focused subnet may prioritize transparency and traceability. The ability to tailor subnets to specific industry needs opens doors to a wide range of decentralized applications catering to diverse sectors.

Community-driven Subnets: Communities within the ICP DAO ecosystem have the autonomy to create their own subnets, fostering community-driven initiatives and projects. These community-driven subnets can range from social impact initiatives to collaborative efforts in the arts and entertainment industry. The decentralized and customizable nature of subnets empowers communities to shape their own decentralized destinies.

Conclusion: Subnets as Pillars of a Scalable and Diverse ICP DAO Ecosystem

In the expansive canvas of the Internet Computer Protocol DAO system, subnets emerge as foundational pillars, fostering diversity, scalability, and resilience. The modular architecture of subnets empowers communities and industries to define their own governance models and rules, while interconnectivity ensures a collaborative and innovative decentralized ecosystem. As we journey through the technological foundations of ICP DAOs, subnets stand as a testament to the adaptability and forward-thinking design principles that underpin the decentralized future envisioned by the ICP protocol. In the subsequent chapters, we will delve deeper into the mechanics of ICP DAOs, exploring governance tokenomics, the evolution of decentralized decision-making, and the real-world impact of community-driven initiatives within the ICP DAO ecosystem.

Chapter 2: The Mechanics of ICP DAOs
Proposal Creation and Voting Process: Empowering Community Participation

In the decentralized realm of Internet Computer Protocol (ICP) DAOs, the ability for participants to actively shape the trajectory of the network is fundamental. Proposal creation and the subsequent voting process form the bedrock of decentralized decision-making, empowering community participation and fostering a sense of ownership within the ICP DAO ecosystem. This section explores the intricacies of proposal creation and the voting process, shedding light on how these mechanisms drive community engagement, shape governance, and contribute to the evolution of the decentralized landscape.

The Essence of Community-Driven Proposals

Decentralized Governance as a Collaborative Endeavor: At the heart of ICP DAOs lies the principle of decentralized governance—a departure from traditional centralized models where decisions are made by a select few. In the ICP DAO ecosystem, governance is a collaborative endeavor where participants, holding governance tokens, have the agency to propose changes, upgrades, or initiatives that impact the network. Proposal creation becomes the vehicle through which community members actively contribute to the evolution of the decentralized network.

The Power of Proposals: Proposals within ICP DAOs encapsulate the collective will and vision of the community. They can range from technical upgrades to changes in governance rules, from the introduction of new features to community-driven initiatives. The power of proposals lies in their ability to democratize decision-making, allowing diverse perspectives and ideas to be considered and implemented based on the consensus of the community.

Navigating the Proposal Landscape

Proposal Submission: The journey of a proposal begins with its submission to the ICP DAO network. Any participant holding governance tokens can initiate a proposal, and the decentralized nature of the network ensures that the process is open and accessible. Proposals can originate from individual community members, development teams, or even collaborations between subnets, showcasing the versatility and inclusivity of the ICP DAO ecosystem.

Clarity and Transparency in Proposal Content: Clear and transparent communication is paramount in the world of decentralized governance. A well-crafted proposal outlines the purpose, scope, and expected impact of the suggested change or initiative. Whether it pertains to technical upgrades, changes in parameters, or the allocation of resources, the proposal content serves as a guide for the community to evaluate and make informed decisions during the subsequent voting process.

The Dynamics of Voting: A Democratic Process

Token-based Voting: Once a proposal is submitted, the community engages in a democratic process of decision-making through token-based voting. Governance token holders are granted voting power proportional to the number of tokens they possess. This token-based voting model ensures that those who have a significant stake in the network have a proportional say in its governance, aligning with the principles of stakeholder influence in decentralized systems.

Voting Period and Quorums: The voting process unfolds over a specified period, allowing participants sufficient time to review, discuss, and cast their votes. Quorums, or minimum participation thresholds, may be set to ensure that proposals are subject to a meaningful level of community engagement. This mechanism safeguards against low participation scenarios where decisions could be made by a disproportionately small number of voters.

Types of Votes and Decision Outcomes

Binary and Multi-option Votes: ICP DAOs offer flexibility in the types of votes that can occur. Binary votes involve a straightforward decision between two options, such as approving or rejecting a proposal. Multi-option votes, on the other hand, allow the community to choose from multiple proposed options, introducing a layer of nuance and complexity to decision-making. This flexibility accommodates a diverse range of proposals, each with its own unique context and considerations.

Decision Outcomes: The outcome of a vote determines the fate of the proposal. If a proposal garners sufficient support, it moves forward for implementation. On the contrary, if it fails to meet the required approval threshold, it is rejected. The transparent nature of the voting process ensures that the community is informed about the decision outcomes, promoting accountability and trust within the ICP DAO ecosystem.

Empowering Community Participation through Governance Tokens

Tokenomics and Participation: The distribution and utilization of governance tokens play a pivotal role in empowering community participation. Governance tokens serve as a form of economic stake in the network, aligning the interests of participants with the success and stability of the ICP DAO ecosystem. The possession of governance tokens not only grants voting power but also symbolizes a commitment to the network's well-being and a desire to actively contribute to its governance.

Incentivizing Participation: Incentives are crucial in driving community engagement. ICP DAOs may introduce mechanisms to incentivize active participation in the proposal creation and voting process. This could include rewards for voting, additional governance token allocations for contributors, or other incentive structures designed to encourage meaningful contributions to the decentralized governance of the network.

Challenges and Considerations in the Proposal and Voting Mechanism

Ensuring Security and Integrity: The decentralized nature of ICP DAOs brings both opportunities and challenges. Security and integrity considerations are paramount to safeguard against potential attacks, manipulation, or collusion. Measures such as secure voting mechanisms, encryption, and robust identity verification contribute to the overall security of the proposal and voting process.

Addressing Voter Apathy: Community engagement is a continuous challenge in decentralized governance. Voter apathy, where token holders abstain from participating in the voting process, can impact the effectiveness of decentralized decision-making. Strategies such as awareness campaigns, educational initiatives, and ongoing community involvement efforts may be employed to address this challenge and foster a culture of active participation.

Real-world Impact: Proposals in Action

Technical Upgrades and Protocol Enhancements: Proposals within ICP DAOs often focus on technical upgrades and protocol enhancements. These could include optimizations to the underlying blockchain infrastructure, improvements to consensus mechanisms, or the integration of cutting-edge technologies. The ability for the community to actively propose and vote on technical changes ensures that the ICP DAO ecosystem remains dynamic and responsive to technological advancements.

Community-driven Initiatives: Beyond technical considerations, proposals frequently encompass community-driven initiatives. These could range from partnerships with external organizations to collaborative projects between subnets. The decentralized decision-making process allows for the exploration and implementation of initiatives that align with the values and goals of the community.

Conclusion: Democratizing Decisions, Shaping the Future

In the decentralized tapestry of ICP DAOs, proposal creation and the voting process stand as powerful tools for democratizing decisions and shaping the future of the network. Community participation, fueled by governance tokens and incentivized by a shared commitment to the network's success, becomes the driving force behind the evolution of decentralized governance. As we navigate through the mechanics of ICP DAOs, the next chapters will unveil further layers of governance tokenomics, the adaptive evolution of decentralized decision-making, and the real-world impact of community-driven initiatives within the ICP DAO ecosystem.

Governance Tokenomics: Aligning Incentives and Empowering DAOs

In the decentralized landscape of Internet Computer Protocol (ICP) DAOs, governance tokenomics plays a pivotal role in shaping the dynamics of decision-making, incentivizing active participation, and empowering the decentralized autonomous organizations (DAOs) within the ecosystem. This section delves into the intricacies of governance tokenomics, exploring how the design, distribution, and utilization of governance tokens align incentives, foster community engagement, and contribute to the flourishing of DAOs within the ICP network.

The Significance of Governance Tokens

Defining Governance Tokens: At the core of decentralized governance within ICP DAOs are governance tokens. These tokens serve a dual purpose—representing a form of economic stake in the network and providing voting power to their holders. Governance tokens align the interests of participants with the success and stability of the ICP DAO ecosystem, creating a symbiotic relationship between economic incentives and active engagement in decentralized decision-making.

Tokenomics as the Economic Engine: Governance tokenomics encompasses the economic principles and mechanisms that govern the distribution, circulation, and utility of governance tokens. It is the economic engine that propels the decentralized governance of ICP DAOs, driving meaningful participation, influencing decision outcomes, and shaping the long-term sustainability of the network.

Distribution of Governance Tokens

Ensuring Fair Distribution: A fair and transparent distribution of governance tokens is paramount to the integrity of decentralized governance. ICP DAOs often implement strategies to ensure widespread access to governance tokens, avoiding concentrations of power and fostering a more inclusive decision-making process. Initial token distribution methods, such as airdrops, token sales, or community grants, contribute to the equitable allocation of governance tokens among participants.

Community Participation and Token Allocation: Governance tokens are often distributed to those actively participating in the ICP DAO ecosystem. This participation can take various forms, including proposal creation, voting, contributing to the development of the network, or engaging in community initiatives. Token allocations based on participation incentivize community members to contribute meaningfully to the growth and governance of the network.

Utility of Governance Tokens

Voting Power and Decision-making: The primary utility of governance tokens lies in the voting power they confer to their holders. The more governance tokens an individual possesses, the greater their influence in decentralized decision-making. This aligns with the principle of stakeholder governance, where those with a significant economic stake in the network have a proportional say in shaping its future.

Governance Beyond Voting: Governance tokens often extend beyond voting and play a role in shaping other aspects of the decentralized ecosystem. They may be used for staking, liquidity provision, or access to specific features and functionalities within the network. This multi-faceted utility enhances the value proposition of governance tokens, making them integral to various activities and mechanisms within the ICP DAO ecosystem.

Aligning Incentives for Active Participation

Incentivizing Proposal Creation: Governance tokens serve as powerful incentives for community members to actively participate in the proposal creation process. Individuals who propose meaningful changes, upgrades, or initiatives that receive community support can be rewarded with additional governance tokens. This aligns the economic interests of participants with the proactive enhancement and evolution of the ICP DAO network.

Rewarding Voting Participation: Active participation in the voting process is crucial for the effectiveness of decentralized decision-making. Governance tokenomics includes mechanisms to reward individuals who consistently engage in voting. This could take the form of additional governance token allocations, exclusive access to network features, or other incentives designed to acknowledge and encourage ongoing participation.

Dynamic Governance Token Models

Evolving Tokenomics Models: The design of governance tokenomics is not static; it evolves over time to adapt to the changing needs and dynamics of the ICP DAO ecosystem. Tokenomics models may undergo upgrades, incorporating feedback from the community and addressing challenges that arise during the network's growth. This adaptability ensures that governance tokenomics remains a robust and responsive framework for aligning incentives and empowering DAOs.

Token Burns and Supply Adjustments: Token burns, or the permanent removal of a portion of circulating tokens, can be employed as a mechanism to adjust token supply and maintain scarcity. This practice can contribute to the long-term value appreciation of governance tokens. Supply adjustments may also be implemented through community-driven governance proposals, allowing participants to collectively decide on changes to the tokenomics structure.

Challenges and Considerations in Governance Tokenomics

Avoiding Token Concentration: Token concentration among a small number of entities poses a risk to the decentralization and resilience of ICP DAOs. Governance tokenomics should include measures to prevent excessive concentration of tokens in the hands of a few, such as implementing token vesting schedules, strategic distribution mechanisms, or limitations on token accumulation.

Balancing Incentives and Sustainability: Aligning incentives for active participation is crucial, but it must be balanced with the long-term sustainability of the ICP DAO ecosystem. Overemphasis on short-term incentives may lead to unsustainable tokenomics models. Striking the right balance ensures that governance tokenomics remains resilient, adaptive, and capable of fostering continuous community engagement.

Real-world Impact: Empowering DAOs

Decentralized Development Funding: Governance tokens empower DAOs within the ICP network to fund development initiatives in a decentralized manner. Proposals for technical upgrades, protocol enhancements, or community-driven projects can secure funding through the allocation of governance tokens. This decentralized development funding model accelerates innovation and ensures that the priorities of the community drive the evolution of the network.

Community-driven Initiatives: Governance tokens enable the initiation and execution of community-driven initiatives. Whether it's the creation of educational programs, partnerships with external organizations, or social impact projects, governance tokens serve as the economic fuel that powers these initiatives. The ability to align economic incentives with community-driven goals fosters a culture of innovation and collaboration within the ICP DAO ecosystem.

Conclusion: Tokenomics as the Cornerstone of Decentralized Governance

In the intricate web of ICP DAOs, governance tokenomics stands as the cornerstone of decentralized governance, aligning incentives, and empowering DAOs within the ecosystem. The thoughtful distribution, utility, and evolution of governance tokens create a dynamic framework that fosters active participation, drives decision-making, and contributes to the sustainable growth of the ICP DAO network. As we navigate through the mechanics of ICP DAOs, subsequent chapters will unravel further layers of decentralized decision-making, explore the adaptive evolution of governance mechanisms, and delve into the real-world impact of community-driven initiatives within the ICP DAO ecosystem.

DAO Evolution and Adaptation: Embracing the Dynamic Landscape

Decentralized Autonomous Organizations (DAOs) within the Internet Computer Protocol (ICP) ecosystem are not static entities; rather, they are dynamic systems designed to evolve and adapt to the ever-changing landscape of decentralized governance. This section delves into the mechanisms that drive the evolution of DAOs, exploring their adaptive nature, resilience to change, and the continuous process of improvement that characterizes these decentralized entities.

The Living Nature of DAOs

Decentralized Governance as an Iterative Process: One of the defining features of DAOs within the ICP network is their iterative nature. Decentralized governance is not a one-time event but an ongoing process of evolution and adaptation. DAOs are designed to learn from experiences, incorporate feedback from the community, and continuously improve their structures, mechanisms, and decision-making processes.

Adaptability to Technological Advancements: Technology is in a perpetual state of advancement, and DAOs must adapt to harness the benefits of these advancements. The ICP DAO ecosystem is built upon a foundation that embraces technological innovation. DAOs evolve in tandem with advancements in smart contract capabilities, consensus mechanisms, and other technological enhancements that contribute to the efficiency, security, and functionality of the ICP network.

The Mechanisms of DAO Evolution

Community-Driven Proposals for DAO Improvement: One of the primary mechanisms driving DAO evolution is the submission of community-driven proposals aimed at enhancing the DAO's structure or functionality. These proposals can cover a spectrum of improvements, including changes to governance mechanisms, upgrades to smart contract functionality, or adjustments to the DAO's tokenomics. The decentralized nature of proposal creation ensures that any community member can contribute ideas for DAO evolution.

Voting on DAO Upgrades: The decision-making process for DAO evolution relies on the collective wisdom of the community. Governance token holders participate in the voting process to determine whether proposed upgrades should be implemented. This democratic approach ensures that DAO evolution aligns with the preferences and interests of the majority of stakeholders. Successful votes result in the implementation of upgrades, marking a milestone in the continuous evolution of DAOs.

Continuous Improvement of Governance Models

Iterative Governance Design: Governance models within DAOs are not set in stone; they undergo iterative design processes to enhance their effectiveness and responsiveness. The continuous improvement of governance models involves experimenting with different decision-making mechanisms, voting structures, and incentive systems. Community feedback and data-driven insights play a crucial role in shaping governance models that are resilient, transparent, and aligned with the evolving needs of the DAO.

Experimentation with Decentralized Decision-making: Decentralized decision-making is a dynamic field, and DAOs serve as laboratories for experimentation. DAOs may explore novel decision-making mechanisms, such as quadratic voting, futarchy, or liquid democracy, to assess their suitability for the decentralized landscape. Experimentation allows DAOs to identify models that align with their goals and the values of their community, fostering a culture of innovation within the decentralized governance space.

Incorporating Feedback Loops for Continuous Learning

Community Feedback Mechanisms: The incorporation of feedback loops is instrumental in the continuous learning and improvement of DAOs. Various mechanisms, such as community forums, governance forums, and decentralized communication channels, enable stakeholders to provide feedback on the performance of DAOs, suggest improvements, and engage in discussions about the future direction of the decentralized entity.

Data-driven Decision-making: DAOs leverage data analytics and metrics to assess the impact of implemented changes and the overall performance of the decentralized governance system. Data-driven decision-making enables DAOs to make informed choices based on empirical evidence, fostering a culture of transparency, accountability, and adaptability. Insights from data analysis contribute to the refinement of governance mechanisms and the identification of areas for improvement.

Community-driven Initiatives: The Heartbeat of DAO Evolution

Empowering Community-Driven Projects: Beyond governance changes, DAOs often play a central role in empowering and supporting community-driven initiatives.

These initiatives can take various forms, including development projects, educational programs, partnerships, or social impact campaigns. DAOs allocate resources, often in the form of governance tokens, to fund and accelerate community-driven projects, catalyzing innovation and collaboration within the ICP ecosystem.

Decentralized Development Funding: DAOs act as decentralized funding mechanisms for development projects that contribute to the growth and improvement of the ICP network. Community members can propose projects, request funding in the form of governance tokens, and, through the voting process, secure the necessary resources to bring their ideas to fruition. This decentralized development funding model ensures that the broader community has a say in prioritizing projects that align with the collective vision of the DAO.

Addressing Challenges and Navigating DAO Evolution

Security and Resilience: As DAOs evolve, ensuring the security and resilience of the decentralized governance system becomes paramount. DAOs must navigate potential vulnerabilities, security risks, and external threats. Continuous security audits, robust smart contract development practices, and community-driven initiatives for the identification and mitigation of risks contribute to the overall security posture of DAOs.

Addressing Governance Apathy: Maintaining active community engagement is an ongoing challenge in DAO evolution. The phenomenon of governance apathy, where stakeholders disengage from decision-making processes, can impact the effectiveness of DAOs. Strategies such as awareness campaigns, educational initiatives, and the creation of compelling incentives for participation contribute to overcoming governance apathy and fostering a culture of active involvement.

Real-world Impact: DAOs in Action

Evolution in Response to Market Dynamics: DAOs within the ICP network showcase their adaptive nature in response to market dynamics. Changes in market conditions, technological advancements, or shifts in community priorities can prompt DAOs to propose and implement adjustments to their governance structures. This agility allows DAOs to remain relevant and effective in the ever-changing landscape of decentralized finance and governance.

Community-driven Social Impact Initiatives: The adaptive nature of DAOs is exemplified in their support for community-driven social impact initiatives. DAOs allocate resources to projects focused on social good, ranging from environmental sustainability efforts to initiatives addressing social inequality. This community-driven approach to social impact underscores the capacity of DAOs to contribute positively to the broader societal landscape.

Conclusion: A Dynamic Future for DAOs

In the dynamic realm of ICP DAOs, evolution is not just a possibility but an inherent characteristic. DAOs embody a continuous learning process, where feedback loops, community-driven initiatives, and governance adaptations contribute to their resilience and relevance. As we navigate the mechanics of ICP DAOs, the subsequent chapters will unravel further layers of decentralized decision-making, explore governance tokenomics, and delve into the real-world impact of community-driven initiatives within the ICP DAO ecosystem.

Securing ICP DAOs: Protecting Assets and Maintaining Trust

In the intricate landscape of Internet Computer Protocol (ICP) DAOs, security is paramount. As decentralized autonomous organizations, ICP DAOs manage valuable assets, govern decision-making processes, and serve as pillars of trust within the broader community. This section delves into the multifaceted realm of securing ICP DAOs, exploring the measures, protocols, and strategies implemented to protect assets, safeguard against vulnerabilities, and uphold the trust of stakeholders in the decentralized governance ecosystem.

The Stakes of Security in ICP DAOs

Decentralization and Security: Decentralization, the cornerstone of ICP DAOs, introduces a unique set of security considerations. Unlike centralized entities where security measures can be more easily enforced, DAOs rely on distributed networks, smart contracts, and consensus mechanisms. Securing ICP DAOs involves navigating the complexities of a decentralized environment while addressing potential vulnerabilities that could compromise the integrity of the governance system.

Assets at Stake: ICP DAOs manage a spectrum of assets, including governance tokens, funds allocated for community projects, and assets associated with decentralized applications (DApps) and smart contracts. The decentralized nature of these assets requires robust security measures to protect against potential threats such as hacking, fraud, or exploitation of vulnerabilities in the underlying technology.

Foundations of Security in ICP DAOs

Smart Contract Audits: At the heart of many DAOs are smart contracts—self-executing contracts with the terms of the agreement directly written into code. Smart contract audits are a foundational element of securing ICP DAOs. Independent security audits, conducted by reputable firms, help identify vulnerabilities, potential exploits, or coding errors within smart contracts. The aim is to ensure the reliability and security of the code that governs key functionalities of the DAO.

Code Transparency and Open Source Practices: Transparency is a key tenet of security in ICP DAOs. Many DAOs adopt open-source practices, making their code publicly accessible and allowing the broader community to review, analyze, and contribute to the security of the codebase. Code transparency fosters collaboration, enables the identification of potential issues, and builds trust among stakeholders in the DAO.

Governance Security: Protecting Decision-Making Processes

Immutable Governance Records: The immutability of governance records is a security feature that adds trust to the decision-making processes of ICP DAOs. Governance decisions, once executed, become part of the blockchain's immutable ledger. This ensures transparency and accountability, as stakeholders can review past decisions and understand the historical context of governance changes within the DAO.

Decentralized Identity and Access Control: Ensuring the integrity of decision-making requires robust identity and access control mechanisms. Decentralized identity solutions, often built on blockchain technology, help verify the authenticity of participants in the governance process. Access control mechanisms limit the authority of individuals or entities within the DAO based on their level of involvement, preventing unauthorized changes to governance parameters.

Protecting Assets: Wallet Security and Fund Management

Secure Wallet Practices: The security of assets within ICP DAOs begins with the adoption of secure wallet practices. Participants, including DAO members and token holders, are encouraged to use hardware wallets or other secure storage solutions to safeguard their private keys. Wallet security is a critical aspect of protecting assets against unauthorized access, phishing attacks, or other forms of malicious activity.

Multi-Signature Wallets: Many ICP DAOs leverage multi-signature wallets as an additional layer of security for managing funds and making critical decisions. Multi-signature wallets require multiple private keys to authorize transactions, reducing the risk of a single point of failure. This approach enhances security by distributing the responsibility for fund management among multiple key holders.

Continuous Monitoring and Incident Response

Security Monitoring Systems: Continuous monitoring is essential to identify potential security threats in real-time. Security monitoring systems within ICP DAOs track key metrics, such as transaction activity, smart contract interactions, and governance proposals. Anomalies or suspicious behavior trigger alerts, allowing DAOs to respond swiftly to potential security incidents.

Incident Response Plans: Preparedness is a key aspect of security in ICP DAOs. Establishing comprehensive incident response plans ensures that the DAO is ready to address security breaches, unexpected events, or emergent threats. These plans outline the steps to be taken in the event of a security incident, including communication protocols, collaboration with security experts, and potential recovery measures.

Security Audits: A Continuous Process

Regular Security Audits: Security is not a one-time consideration but an ongoing process of assessment and improvement. Regular security audits, conducted by independent third-party experts, help identify new vulnerabilities, assess the effectiveness of existing security measures, and ensure that the DAO's security protocols are aligned with the evolving threat landscape.

Community-driven Security Initiatives: The decentralized nature of ICP DAOs extends to their security measures. Community-driven security initiatives encourage active participation in identifying and addressing potential security risks. Bug bounty programs, where individuals are rewarded for responsibly disclosing security vulnerabilities, exemplify the collaborative approach to security within the decentralized governance ecosystem.

Challenges in Securing ICP DAOs

Dynamic Threat Landscape: The decentralized nature of ICP DAOs exposes them to a dynamic and evolving threat landscape. Security challenges include potential exploits in smart contracts, vulnerabilities in the underlying blockchain infrastructure, and novel attack vectors that may emerge as the technology evolves. Adapting to these challenges requires a proactive and vigilant security posture.

Human Factors: Security is not only a technological consideration but also involves human factors. Risks associated with phishing attacks, social engineering, or human errors in key management can pose significant challenges. Educating participants about secure practices, fostering a culture of security awareness, and implementing user-friendly security measures contribute to mitigating these risks.

Real-world Impact: Building Trust through Security

Stakeholder Confidence: The security practices implemented by ICP DAOs directly influence stakeholder confidence. A secure and resilient DAO not only protects assets but also builds trust among governance participants, token holders, and the broader community. Stakeholder confidence is crucial for the sustainable growth and success of decentralized governance initiatives.

Community Resilience: Security is intertwined with the resilience of the ICP DAO community. The ability to effectively respond to security incidents, recover from potential breaches, and continuously improve security measures fosters resilience. A resilient community is more likely to weather challenges, adapt to changes, and sustain the decentralized governance ecosystem.

Conclusion: Fortifying the Foundations of ICP DAOs

In the dynamic and decentralized landscape of ICP DAOs, security is a foundational pillar that fortifies the integrity of decision-making processes, protects valuable assets, and upholds the trust of stakeholders. As we navigate through the mechanics of ICP DAOs, subsequent chapters will uncover further layers of decentralized decision-making, explore governance tokenomics, and delve into the real-world impact of community-driven initiatives within the ICP DAO ecosystem.

Chapter 3: ICP DAOs in Action: Empowering Real-World Applications

Community-Driven Governance: ICP DAOs in the Realm of Non-Profit Organizations

Decentralized Autonomous Organizations (DAOs) within the Internet Computer Protocol (ICP) ecosystem extend their transformative reach into diverse sectors, and non-profit organizations stand at the forefront of this evolution. In this exploration, we delve into the dynamic landscape of community-driven governance within ICP DAOs, particularly focusing on their impact and potential in the realm of non-profit organizations. From redefining philanthropy to enhancing transparency and community engagement, ICP DAOs are ushering in a new era of decentralized governance that aligns seamlessly with the values and missions of non-profits.

Empowering Non-Profit Organizations through Decentralized Governance

The Evolution of Philanthropy: ICP DAOs are catalyzing a paradigm shift in the realm of philanthropy and non-profit work. Traditional models of charitable giving often involve centralized decision-making by a small group of stakeholders. In contrast, community-driven governance empowers a broader network of contributors to collectively decide on funding priorities, initiatives, and strategic directions for non-profit organizations.

Inclusive Decision-Making: Decentralized governance ensures that decision-making processes are inclusive and representative of the diverse perspectives within the non-profit community. All stakeholders, including donors, beneficiaries, and supporters, have a voice in shaping the direction of non-profit initiatives. This inclusivity fosters a sense of ownership and shared responsibility, aligning the organization's activities with the values and needs of its community.

Community-Driven Funding for Non-Profit Initiatives

Decentralized Development Funding: ICP DAOs provide a powerful mechanism for non-profits to secure decentralized development funding. Through the creation of governance proposals, non-profit organizations can outline their projects, funding requirements, and the expected impact of their initiatives. The broader community, including donors and supporters, can then participate in the governance process to allocate resources to projects aligned with their shared values and philanthropic goals.

Transparency in Resource Allocation: One of the key advantages of leveraging ICP DAOs for non-profit governance is the transparency in resource allocation. The blockchain-based nature of ICP ensures that every transaction and fund allocation is recorded on an immutable ledger. This transparency builds trust among stakeholders, as they can track and verify how resources are utilized, ensuring accountability and ethical financial practices within the non-profit sector.

Enhancing Community Engagement and Participation

Token-Based Incentives for Engagement: To encourage active participation and engagement within the non-profit community, ICP DAOs often incorporate token-based incentives. Donors and supporters who contribute to governance decisions, participate in discussions, or contribute to the success of non-profit initiatives can receive governance tokens as a form of recognition and reward. This incentivization model aligns the interests of the community with the growth and impact of the non-profit organization.

Decentralized Decision-Making in Action: Non-profit organizations utilizing ICP DAOs experience decentralized decision-making in action. Proposals for new initiatives, changes in strategic direction, or resource allocations are submitted to the DAO, and the community engages in a transparent and open voting process. The collective decisions of the community shape the trajectory of the non-profit, reflecting a democratic and community-driven approach to governance.

Facilitating Global Collaboration in Non-Profit Initiatives

Global Reach of ICP DAOs: The decentralized nature of ICP DAOs facilitates global collaboration for non-profit initiatives. Stakeholders from different geographic locations can participate in governance processes, contribute to projects, and engage with the non-profit community. This global reach transcends traditional barriers, enabling a diverse and interconnected network of individuals and organizations to collaborate seamlessly for shared philanthropic goals.

Cross-Border Funding and Impact: ICP DAOs open avenues for cross-border funding and impact within the non-profit sector. Donors and supporters from around the world can contribute to non-profit initiatives without being restricted by geographical constraints. This borderless approach to philanthropy enhances the potential for non-profits to address global challenges, foster international collaboration, and amplify the impact of their initiatives.

Realizing Synergies Between Donors and Beneficiaries

Alignment of Values: Decentralized governance within ICP DAOs fosters a unique alignment of values between donors and beneficiaries in the non-profit sector. The transparent and community-driven decision-making processes ensure that the priorities and needs of the community being served are directly considered in governance decisions. This alignment enhances the effectiveness and sustainability of non-profit initiatives by ensuring that they are rooted in the values and aspirations of those they aim to benefit.

Feedback Loops for Continuous Improvement: ICP DAOs enable the establishment of feedback loops between donors and beneficiaries. The transparent recording of governance decisions and the direct involvement of beneficiaries in the governance process allow for real-time feedback on the impact of non-profit initiatives. This continuous feedback loop contributes to the adaptive evolution of programs, ensuring that they remain responsive to the evolving needs of the community.

Challenges and Considerations in Non-Profit Governance

Navigating Regulatory Environments: The decentralized and borderless nature of ICP DAOs introduces challenges related to navigating diverse regulatory environments. Non-profit organizations must consider the legal and regulatory landscape in different jurisdictions, ensuring compliance with relevant laws while leveraging the advantages of decentralized governance. Collaborative efforts and industry advocacy can play a role in addressing these challenges.

Ensuring Inclusivity: While decentralized governance strives for inclusivity, challenges may arise in ensuring that all voices within a non-profit community are heard. Language barriers, technological accessibility, and varying levels of engagement can impact the inclusivity of governance processes. Non-profits utilizing ICP DAOs need to implement strategies that actively address these challenges and create an inclusive environment for decision-making.

Real-world Impact: Non-Profit Governance in Action

Addressing Global Challenges: ICP DAOs empower non-profit organizations to address a spectrum of global challenges, from environmental sustainability to healthcare and education. The community-driven governance model ensures that solutions are devised collaboratively, drawing on the collective expertise, resources, and passion of a global network of stakeholders. Non-profits leveraging ICP DAOs become catalysts for positive change on a global scale.

Community-led Social Impact Initiatives: The impact of ICP DAOs in non-profit governance extends beyond traditional philanthropy. Community-led social impact initiatives, supported and funded through decentralized governance, create a ripple effect of positive change. These initiatives span areas such as environmental conservation, social justice, and community development, showcasing the transformative potential of decentralized governance in driving grassroots-level impact.

Conclusion: A New Era for Non-Profit Governance

In the dynamic landscape of ICP DAOs, the realm of non-profit governance emerges as a beacon of innovation and collaboration. Community-driven decision-making, borderless collaboration, and the alignment of values between donors and beneficiaries redefine the possibilities for non-profit organizations. As we navigate through the impact of ICP DAOs in the real world, subsequent chapters will unveil further dimensions of decentralized decision-making, explore the intersection of ICP DAOs with decentralized finance (DeFi), and delve into their transformative role in fostering social impact and innovation.

Decentralized Finance (DeFi) and ICP DAOs: Redefining Financial Services

In the dynamic landscape of decentralized autonomous organizations (DAOs) within the Internet Computer Protocol (ICP) ecosystem, the intersection with decentralized finance (DeFi) emerges as a groundbreaking frontier. This section explores the transformative synergy between ICP DAOs and the rapidly evolving realm of decentralized finance, shedding light on how these entities redefine financial services, foster innovation, and democratize access to a broad spectrum of financial opportunities.

The Rise of Decentralized Finance (DeFi)

DeFi as a Paradigm Shift: Decentralized finance, often abbreviated as DeFi, represents a paradigm shift in the traditional financial landscape. Rooted in blockchain technology and smart contracts, DeFi leverages the principles of decentralization to reimagine and reconstruct financial services. The core tenets of DeFi include transparency, accessibility, and the removal of intermediaries, empowering users to interact with financial products and services in a peer-to-peer and trustless manner.

The ICP Ecosystem and DeFi Integration: Within the ICP ecosystem, the integration of decentralized finance is catalyzed by the capabilities of smart contracts, aBFT consensus mechanisms, and the seamless interoperability afforded by the Internet Computer Protocol. ICP DAOs play a pivotal role in this integration, serving as the decentralized entities that govern, fund, and drive innovation within the burgeoning landscape of DeFi applications.

Decentralized Lending and Borrowing

Leveraging Smart Contracts for Loans: ICP DAOs redefine lending and borrowing through the implementation of smart contracts. Smart contract-based lending platforms enable users to access loans without the need for traditional intermediaries. Borrowers can collateralize assets, and through transparent and automated smart contracts, secure loans with predefined terms. This decentralized lending model eliminates the need for banks or financial institutions, providing a trustless and efficient mechanism for accessing capital.

ICP DAOs as Governance Hubs: In the DeFi space, ICP DAOs emerge as governance hubs for decentralized lending protocols. Participants in the ICP community collectively decide on lending parameters, interest rates, and risk management strategies through transparent and community-driven governance processes. This ensures that the lending and borrowing ecosystem aligns with the values, preferences, and risk tolerance of the broader ICP community.

Decentralized Exchanges (DEXs) and Liquidity Pools

Facilitating Trustless Asset Trading: Decentralized exchanges (DEXs) powered by ICP DAOs redefine asset trading by enabling trustless and peer-to-peer transactions. Participants can trade digital assets directly from their wallets without the need for intermediaries. The smart contract infrastructure ensures the transparent execution of trades, and the decentralized nature of DEXs enhances security, reduces counterparty risk, and fosters a permissionless environment for asset exchange.

Liquidity Pools and Automated Market Makers (AMMs): ICP DAOs contribute to the creation and governance of liquidity pools within decentralized exchanges. Liquidity providers contribute assets to pools, facilitating seamless trading by ensuring ample liquidity. Automated Market Makers (AMMs) powered by smart contracts enable decentralized price discovery and trade execution. ICP DAOs play a key role in determining the parameters of liquidity pools and optimizing the functionality of AMMs through community-driven governance.

Tokenization of Assets and Decentralized Fund Management

Tokenizing Real-World Assets: ICP DAOs redefine traditional asset ownership by facilitating the tokenization of real-world assets. Through the issuance of blockchain-based tokens, real estate, art, or other tangible assets can be represented and traded on decentralized platforms. Tokenization enhances liquidity, lowers entry barriers for investors, and enables fractional ownership, democratizing access to a diverse range of assets.

Community-Driven Fund Management: In the realm of decentralized finance, ICP DAOs emerge as pioneers in community-driven fund management. Through governance proposals and voting mechanisms, community members participate in decisions related to asset allocation, investment strategies, and risk management. This democratized approach to fund management ensures that the broader community has a say in shaping the investment landscape within the ICP ecosystem.

Decentralized Derivatives and Prediction Markets

Smart Contract-powered Derivatives: ICP DAOs contribute to the evolution of financial instruments by supporting the development of decentralized derivatives. Smart contracts enable the creation of synthetic assets, options, and other derivative products without reliance on centralized intermediaries. ICP DAOs govern the parameters of decentralized derivatives platforms, ensuring transparency, fairness, and community-driven risk management.

Prediction Markets for Informed Decision-Making: Decentralized prediction markets within the ICP ecosystem empower community members to make informed decisions based on crowd wisdom. ICP DAOs facilitate the creation and governance of prediction markets, where participants can bet on the outcomes of future events. These markets harness collective intelligence, providing valuable insights and serving as decentralized tools for risk hedging and decision-making.

Challenges and Considerations in DeFi Integration

Smart Contract Security: The integration of decentralized finance within the ICP ecosystem necessitates a focus on smart contract security. As DeFi platforms rely on smart contracts for critical functions such as lending, borrowing, and trading, vulnerabilities in smart contract code can pose significant risks. Regular security audits, community-driven initiatives, and best practices in smart contract development mitigate these risks.

Regulatory Considerations: The regulatory landscape surrounding decentralized finance continues to evolve. ICP DAOs and DeFi platforms must navigate regulatory considerations related to Know Your Customer (KYC) requirements, Anti-Money Laundering (AML) compliance, and the classification of digital assets. Engaging with regulatory authorities, industry collaboration, and adopting compliance measures contribute to the long-term sustainability of DeFi integration.

Real-world Impact: Democratizing Finance with ICP DAOs

Financial Inclusion and Accessibility: ICP DAOs redefine financial services by fostering financial inclusion and accessibility. The decentralized nature of DeFi eliminates geographical barriers, allowing individuals worldwide to access a spectrum of financial products and services. ICP DAOs play a crucial role in shaping decentralized finance initiatives that prioritize inclusivity, creating opportunities for individuals who were previously excluded from traditional financial systems.

Community-Led Innovation: The collaboration between ICP DAOs and DeFi fuels community-led innovation in financial services. Community members actively contribute to the development, improvement, and governance of decentralized financial platforms. This bottom-up approach to innovation ensures that financial products and services align with the evolving needs, preferences, and values of the ICP community.

Conclusion: The Future of Finance Unfolding

In the convergence of ICP DAOs and decentralized finance, the future of finance unfolds with unprecedented possibilities. The collaborative governance, transparent protocols, and democratized access to financial services redefine the landscape of traditional finance. As we navigate through the impact of ICP DAOs in the real world, subsequent chapters will unveil further dimensions of decentralized decision-making, explore the potential of ICP DAOs in social impact initiatives, and delve into their role in fostering innovation in the arts and entertainment sector.

Social Impact and Community Initiatives: ICP DAOs for the Greater Good

In the dynamic landscape of decentralized autonomous organizations (DAOs) within the Internet Computer Protocol (ICP) ecosystem, the transformative potential extends beyond finance and governance. This section delves into the realm of social impact and community initiatives, exploring how ICP DAOs serve as catalysts for positive change, foster inclusivity, and empower communities to address pressing global challenges.

Empowering Social Impact through ICP DAOs

Reimagining Philanthropy: ICP DAOs usher in a reimagined approach to philanthropy by democratizing decision-making in the allocation of resources for social impact initiatives. Traditional philanthropic models often involve centralized decision-making by a select few, but ICP DAOs empower a broader community to collectively shape the direction of social impact projects. This community-driven approach ensures that initiatives are aligned with the values and priorities of the diverse stakeholders involved.

Transparent Resource Allocation: One of the core strengths of ICP DAOs in the realm of social impact is the transparency in resource allocation. Every decision, from funding community projects to supporting charitable causes, is recorded on an immutable blockchain. This transparency builds trust among stakeholders, providing a clear view of how resources are utilized and ensuring accountability in social impact initiatives.

Community-Driven Social Initiatives

Community-Led Project Proposals: ICP DAOs serve as incubators for community-led project proposals aimed at addressing social issues. Through transparent governance processes, community members can propose projects that tackle challenges such as environmental conservation, education, healthcare, and poverty alleviation. The decentralized decision-making ensures that the community actively participates in shaping the initiatives that resonate with their values and aspirations.

Inclusive Decision-Making: Inclusivity is a cornerstone of social impact initiatives within the ICP ecosystem. ICP DAOs enable a diverse range of participants, including project creators, beneficiaries, and supporters, to have a voice in decision-making. This inclusive approach ensures that the solutions devised are representative of the needs and perspectives of the communities they aim to serve, fostering a sense of ownership and shared responsibility.

Environmental Sustainability and Conservation

Blockchain for Environmental Impact: ICP DAOs contribute to environmental sustainability by leveraging blockchain technology for positive impact. The transparent and verifiable nature of blockchain transactions ensures accountability in environmental initiatives. DAOs can fund projects related to carbon offsetting, reforestation efforts, and sustainable practices, with the community actively participating in the decision-making processes that shape the direction of these projects.

Decentralized Environmental Funds: ICP DAOs play a crucial role in the creation and governance of decentralized environmental funds. These funds can be used to support projects that promote clean energy, biodiversity conservation, and ecological restoration. Through community-driven decision-making, stakeholders within the ICP ecosystem collaboratively determine the allocation of resources to environmental initiatives that align with their shared commitment to sustainability.

Education and Knowledge-Sharing Initiatives

Empowering Education through DAOs: ICP DAOs empower education initiatives by providing a decentralized platform for the creation and support of educational projects. These projects can range from online learning platforms to initiatives that promote literacy and skills development. Through community-driven governance, participants can champion educational causes, allocate resources to impactful projects, and foster a culture of continuous learning within the ICP ecosystem.

Knowledge-Sharing DAOs: ICP DAOs dedicated to knowledge-sharing create a collaborative environment where community members can contribute, curate, and disseminate information. These DAOs facilitate the creation of decentralized knowledge repositories, educational resources, and open-access materials. The transparent and community-driven nature of these initiatives ensures that knowledge-sharing aligns with the diverse needs and interests of the community.

Healthcare and Community Wellness

Decentralized Healthcare Initiatives: ICP DAOs are at the forefront of decentralized healthcare initiatives, redefining how communities approach healthcare and wellness. Community-driven governance allows stakeholders to support projects related to telemedicine, public health awareness, and healthcare access. Transparent decision-making ensures that healthcare initiatives are inclusive and responsive to the unique healthcare challenges faced by different communities.

Wellness DAOs: Wellness DAOs within the ICP ecosystem focus on holistic community well-being. These DAOs may support initiatives related to mental health, fitness, and lifestyle improvements. Through decentralized governance, community members actively contribute to shaping wellness programs and initiatives that resonate with their individual and collective health goals.

Community Engagement and Social Tokenomics

Token-Based Incentives for Social Impact: ICP DAOs leverage token-based incentives to encourage active participation in social impact initiatives. Participants contributing to the success of community projects, volunteering, or championing social causes can earn governance tokens as a form of recognition and reward. This tokenomics model aligns the interests of the community with the success of social impact initiatives, fostering sustained engagement.

Decentralized Social Funding: ICP DAOs facilitate decentralized social funding models where community members collectively contribute to support social impact projects. Social funding DAOs can pool resources to address urgent community needs, respond to disasters, or fund initiatives that bring about positive change. The transparent and democratic nature of these funding mechanisms ensures that the broader community has a say in prioritizing and supporting social causes.

Challenges and Considerations in Social Impact Initiatives

Balancing Global and Local Needs: One of the challenges in social impact initiatives within the ICP ecosystem is finding a balance between global and local needs. Decentralized decision-making processes must consider the unique challenges faced by different communities while fostering a shared commitment to global goals. Community-driven governance mechanisms need to be adaptable and responsive to diverse social contexts.

Ensuring Long-Term Sustainability: The long-term sustainability of social impact initiatives relies on continued community engagement and resource allocation. ICP DAOs must address challenges related to maintaining community interest, ensuring ongoing funding for projects, and adapting to evolving social needs. Sustainable social impact requires a commitment to iterative improvement, community resilience, and a shared vision for the greater good.

Real-world Impact: Transformative Change through ICP DAOs

Positive Change on a Global Scale: ICP DAOs emerge as vehicles for transformative change on a global scale. From environmental sustainability to education and healthcare, the community-driven nature of ICP DAOs ensures that positive change is not confined to geographical boundaries. The real-world impact of these initiatives showcases the potential of decentralized governance to address pressing global challenges and foster collective well-being.

Empowering Local Communities: ICP DAOs empower local communities by giving them a voice in shaping their own destinies. Through community-driven social impact initiatives, local stakeholders actively participate in decision-making processes that directly influence the well-being of their communities. This bottom-up approach fosters a sense of empowerment, ownership, and resilience within localities.

Conclusion: Shaping a Better Future with ICP DAOs

In the dynamic intersection of ICP DAOs and social impact initiatives, the potential for shaping a better future comes to the forefront. Community-driven governance, transparent decision-making, and decentralized social funding redefine how communities address challenges and contribute to positive change. As we navigate through the impact of ICP DAOs in the real world, subsequent chapters will unveil further dimensions of decentralized decision-making, explore the intersection of ICP DAOs with the arts and entertainment sector, and delve into their transformative role in fostering innovation and creativity.

Unlocking Creativity and Innovation: ICP DAOs in the Arts and Entertainment

In the dynamic landscape of decentralized autonomous organizations (DAOs) within the Internet Computer Protocol (ICP) ecosystem, the convergence with the arts and entertainment sector becomes a vibrant tapestry of creativity and innovation. This section explores how ICP DAOs serve as catalysts for transformative change in the arts and entertainment industry, fostering collaboration, empowering creators, and reshaping the way audiences engage with content.

The Transformative Intersection of ICP DAOs and the Arts

Decentralized Collaboration in Creative Industries: ICP DAOs redefine collaboration within creative industries by providing a decentralized platform for artists, musicians, filmmakers, and other creators to collaborate on projects. The transparent and community-driven nature of DAOs ensures that decisions related to project funding, intellectual property, and creative direction are made collectively, fostering a collaborative environment that transcends traditional boundaries.

Incentivizing Creative Contributions: ICP DAOs leverage token-based incentives to reward creative contributions. Artists and creators can receive governance tokens for their work, providing a tangible and decentralized form of recognition. This incentivization model aligns the interests of creators with the success of creative projects, fostering a vibrant ecosystem of contributors within the ICP arts and entertainment community.

Decentralized Funding for Creative Projects

Empowering Independent Creators: ICP DAOs empower independent creators by providing decentralized funding mechanisms for creative projects. Through governance proposals, creators can outline their projects, funding requirements, and the potential impact of their work. The broader community, including art enthusiasts and supporters, can participate in the governance process to allocate resources to projects aligned with their shared artistic interests.

Transparent Funding for the Arts: One of the strengths of ICP DAOs in the arts and entertainment sector is the transparency in funding. Every contribution and fund allocation is recorded on the immutable ICP blockchain, providing a transparent record of financial transactions. This transparency builds trust among stakeholders, ensuring that creators and supporters have visibility into how resources are utilized in the development of artistic projects.

NFTs and Digital Ownership in the Arts

Tokenizing Digital Art: ICP DAOs contribute to the tokenization of digital art, bringing the principles of non-fungible tokens (NFTs) to the forefront of the arts and entertainment industry. Artists can tokenize their digital creations, providing a unique and verifiable representation of ownership on the ICP blockchain. NFTs enable creators to monetize their work, establish digital scarcity, and engage directly with a global audience.

Community-Driven Digital Collectibles: ICP DAOs facilitate the creation and governance of community-driven digital collectibles. Through decentralized decision-making, community members can collectively decide on the creation and distribution of digital assets, fostering a sense of ownership and participation. These digital collectibles can range from virtual art pieces to unique experiences, creating new avenues for artists to connect with their audience.

Decentralized Music and Entertainment Platforms

Decentralized Music Streaming: ICP DAOs reshape the music industry by supporting decentralized music streaming platforms. Artists can release their music on blockchain-based platforms, and the community participates in governance decisions related to content curation, revenue distribution, and platform features. This decentralized approach ensures fair compensation for artists and a democratic approach to shaping the future of music distribution.

Community-Driven Entertainment Experiences: ICP DAOs extend their impact to the entertainment sector by enabling community-driven decision-making in the creation of immersive experiences. From virtual reality concerts to interactive storytelling, decentralized governance ensures that entertainment initiatives are tailored to the preferences of the community. The audience becomes an active participant in shaping the content they consume, leading to a more engaging and inclusive entertainment landscape.

Decentralized Governance for Artistic Organizations

Decentralized Arts Organizations: ICP DAOs support the establishment of decentralized arts organizations that operate on principles of transparent governance. These organizations, ranging from art galleries to cultural institutions, leverage decentralized decision-making for curatorial decisions, exhibition funding, and community engagement initiatives. The collaborative nature of DAOs ensures that artistic organizations remain responsive to the evolving needs and interests of their communities.

Decentralized Film Production: ICP DAOs play a transformative role in the film industry by supporting decentralized film production models. Filmmakers can propose projects to the community, outlining their creative vision, budgetary needs, and potential impact. Through community-driven governance, stakeholders participate in decisions related to film funding, distribution, and collaborative production processes, fostering a decentralized and inclusive approach to filmmaking.

Challenges and Considerations in Decentralized Arts and Entertainment

Intellectual Property and Licensing: The integration of ICP DAOs in the arts and entertainment sector raises questions about intellectual property rights and licensing. Creators and stakeholders must navigate the decentralized landscape to establish clear frameworks for ownership, licensing agreements, and the protection of intellectual property. Collaborative efforts between artists, legal experts, and the wider community are essential to address these challenges.

Adoption and Accessibility: While decentralized models offer transformative potential, challenges related to adoption and accessibility persist. Creators and audiences need user-friendly interfaces, educational resources, and seamless onboarding processes to participate in decentralized arts and entertainment initiatives. The development of accessible tools and platforms is crucial to ensuring widespread adoption and inclusivity.

Real-world Impact: Redefining the Arts with ICP DAOs

Empowering Diverse Creativity: ICP DAOs redefine the arts by empowering a diverse range of creators to contribute to the cultural landscape. From visual artists to musicians and filmmakers, the decentralized nature of DAOs ensures that creative expression flourishes without traditional gatekeepers. This empowerment of diverse creativity leads to a rich and varied artistic ecosystem that resonates with global audiences.

Community-Driven Artistic Renaissance: The intersection of ICP DAOs and the arts sparks a community-driven artistic renaissance. The collaborative decision-making processes foster a sense of shared ownership and participation in the creative process. This renaissance transcends geographic boundaries, allowing artists and audiences from around the world to engage in a global dialogue and contribute to a decentralized and dynamic cultural movement.

Conclusion: A New Era of Artistic Expression

In the convergence of ICP DAOs and the arts and entertainment sector, a new era of artistic expression unfolds. Community-driven governance, transparent funding mechanisms, and decentralized models of ownership redefine how creativity is fostered, shared, and appreciated. As we navigate through the impact of ICP DAOs in the real world, subsequent chapters will unveil further dimensions of decentralized decision-making, explore the potential of ICP DAOs in addressing legal and regulatory considerations, and delve into their role in shaping the future of decentralized governance.

Chapter 4: The Future of ICP DAOs: A Vision for Decentralized Governance

Evolving Governance Models: ICP DAOs as a Paradigm for Modern Governance

In the ever-evolving landscape of decentralized autonomous organizations (DAOs) within the Internet Computer Protocol (ICP) ecosystem, the concept of governance takes center stage as a driving force behind the transformative potential of these decentralized entities. This section explores the evolution of governance models within ICP DAOs, their impact on decision-making processes, and their role as a paradigm for modern governance in the digital age.

The Evolution of Governance in ICP DAOs

Foundations of Decentralized Governance: At the core of ICP DAOs lies the foundational principle of decentralized governance, a departure from traditional hierarchical structures. Governance within DAOs refers to the processes and mechanisms by which decisions are made, rules are established, and the direction of the organization is determined. The evolution of governance models within ICP DAOs reflects a commitment to transparency, inclusivity, and community-driven decision-making.

Smart Contracts and Governance Protocols: ICP DAOs leverage smart contracts to encode and automate governance protocols. These smart contracts, running on the Internet Computer Protocol, enable transparent and programmable decision-making. Through governance protocols, community members participate in proposing, discussing, and voting on decisions that shape the trajectory of the DAO. This technological foundation ensures that governance processes are tamper-resistant, auditable, and enforceable.

Community-Driven Decision-Making

Decentralized Proposal Mechanisms: ICP DAOs embrace decentralized proposal mechanisms as the cornerstone of community-driven decision-making. Community members can submit proposals outlining changes, initiatives, or decisions that require collective input. The transparent nature of proposals ensures that the community has visibility into the issues at hand, fostering an informed and engaged participant base.

Transparent Voting Mechanisms: Voting mechanisms within ICP DAOs are designed to be transparent, secure, and inclusive. Community members can cast votes based on their stake or reputation within the DAO. The use of blockchain technology ensures the integrity of the voting process, preventing manipulation or fraud. Transparent voting mechanisms empower the community to actively participate in decisions related to funding, protocol upgrades, and strategic directions.

Tokenomics and Governance Participation

Incentivizing Governance Participation: ICP DAOs integrate tokenomics to incentivize active governance participation. Governance tokens are distributed to community members who actively contribute to decision-making processes. These tokens represent a form of ownership and influence within the DAO. By aligning the interests of participants with the success of the organization, tokenomics encourages sustained engagement and commitment to the DAO's objectives.

Governance Tokenomics Models: Various governance tokenomics models exist within the ICP ecosystem, each with its unique approach to incentivizing participation. Some DAOs adopt continuous token distributions, rewarding ongoing contributions, while others utilize snapshot mechanisms, capturing a specific moment in time to distribute governance tokens. The diversity of tokenomics models reflects the adaptability of ICP DAOs to different community structures and goals.

Decentralized Identity and Reputation Systems

Ensuring Authentic Participation: Decentralized identity and reputation systems play a crucial role in ensuring the authenticity of participants in ICP DAO governance. Through these systems, participants establish a verifiable and unique digital identity, preventing sybil attacks and ensuring that each participant has a genuine stake in the community. Reputation systems further enhance governance by valuing the contributions and expertise of long-term, trusted community members.

Reputation as a Governance Metric: ICP DAOs often incorporate reputation as a metric in governance decision-making. Participants with a higher reputation score may have increased voting power or influence in shaping the direction of the DAO. This approach recognizes the value of expertise, commitment, and positive contributions, creating a meritocratic governance system that aligns with the principles of decentralized decision-making.

Challenges and Considerations in Decentralized Governance

Balancing Decentralization and Efficiency: Decentralized governance models face the challenge of balancing the principles of decentralization with the need for efficient decision-making. As the community grows, decision-making processes may become more complex, requiring scalable governance solutions. Striking the right balance between decentralization and efficiency is crucial to the long-term sustainability of ICP DAOs.

Mitigating Governance Attacks: ICP DAOs must be resilient to governance attacks, where malicious actors attempt to manipulate decision-making processes for personal gain. Governance attacks can take various forms, including vote-buying, collusion, or manipulation of proposal mechanisms. Robust security measures, transparent governance processes, and community vigilance are essential to mitigate the risk of governance attacks.

Real-world Impact: Democratizing Decision-Making

Empowering a Global Community: ICP DAOs redefine governance by empowering a global community to participate in decision-making processes. The decentralized nature of governance ensures that individuals from diverse backgrounds, geographies, and expertise contribute to shaping the trajectory of the DAO. This global participation fosters a rich tapestry of perspectives and ideas, leading to more robust and resilient decision-making.

Community-Led Innovation: Decentralized governance within ICP DAOs catalyzes community-led innovation. By providing a platform for transparent and inclusive decision-making, DAOs become hubs for creative solutions, iterative improvements, and the exploration of new possibilities. The community-led innovation facilitated by decentralized governance extends beyond the DAO itself, influencing the broader ecosystem and contributing to the evolution of decentralized technologies.

Conclusion: Shaping Modern Governance with ICP DAOs

In the evolution of governance models within ICP DAOs, a vision for modern governance emerges—one that is transparent, inclusive, and community-driven. As we explore the impact of decentralized decision-making, subsequent chapters will unveil further dimensions of ICP DAOs in addressing scalability and sustainability challenges, examine their role in interoperability and ecosystem integration, and delve into their potential as tools for inclusive governance at the individual and community levels.

Scalability and Sustainability: Addressing the Challenges of Growth

In envisioning the future of decentralized autonomous organizations (DAOs) within the Internet Computer Protocol (ICP) ecosystem, scalability and sustainability emerge as pivotal considerations. This section explores the challenges and solutions associated with the growth of ICP DAOs, delving into strategies to ensure scalability, maintain network resilience, and foster sustainable development within the decentralized governance framework.

The Imperative of Scalability in ICP DAOs

Foundations of Scalability: Scalability is a fundamental consideration in the evolution of ICP DAOs. As these decentralized entities attract a growing number of participants and handle an increasing volume of transactions, the underlying infrastructure must be capable of scaling to meet demand. The foundations of scalability in ICP DAOs involve addressing technical, organizational, and economic aspects to accommodate the evolving needs of a burgeoning ecosystem.

Technological Innovations for Scalability: ICP DAOs leverage technological innovations to enhance scalability. The use of sharding, a technique that divides the network into smaller, more manageable parts (shards), allows for parallel processing of transactions. This approach significantly increases the throughput of the ICP network, ensuring that DAOs can handle a larger number of transactions without compromising speed or efficiency.

Navigating the Trilemma: Scalability, Security, and Decentralization

The Scalability-Security-Decentralization Trilemma: In the pursuit of scalability, ICP DAOs must navigate the well-known trilemma—balancing scalability, security, and decentralization. The trilemma posits that achieving high levels of scalability without compromising security or decentralization is a formidable challenge. ICP DAOs employ a range of strategies to strike the right balance, ensuring that the network can scale horizontally while maintaining robust security measures and preserving the decentralized ethos.

Decentralization as a Core Principle: Decentralization remains a core principle in the scalability equation for ICP DAOs. The distributed nature of the Internet Computer Protocol inherently lends itself to decentralization, with nodes across the globe participating in the consensus process. The challenge lies in preserving this decentralization as the network scales, preventing the concentration of power or control in a few entities. Decentralization not only ensures network resilience but also aligns with the democratic principles of DAOs.

Community-Led Scalability Solutions

Governance-Led Scaling Decisions: ICP DAOs embrace a governance-led approach to scaling decisions. Community members actively participate in discussions and decisions related to network upgrades, improvements, and scalability solutions. This decentralized governance model ensures that scaling decisions align with the collective interests and aspirations of the community, fostering a sense of ownership and shared responsibility for the growth of the ICP ecosystem.

Community Validators and Node Operators: The role of community validators and node operators becomes crucial in ensuring the scalability of the ICP network. These participants operate nodes that validate transactions and secure the network. The decentralized nature of these operators prevents a single point of failure and enhances the overall resilience of the ICP ecosystem. Community-led initiatives to onboard and support validators contribute to the scalability and decentralization of the network.

Sustainability in the Decentralized Landscape

Economic Models for Sustainability: As ICP DAOs grow, sustainable economic models become paramount to ensure the long-term viability of the ecosystem. DAOs often employ tokenomics models that align the interests of participants with the success of the organization. Token-based incentives, governance rewards, and mechanisms to capture and redistribute value within the ecosystem contribute to economic sustainability. The challenge lies in designing models that balance incentives, resource allocation, and community-driven decision-making.

Resource Efficiency and Environmental Considerations: Sustainability extends beyond economic models to encompass resource efficiency and environmental considerations. ICP DAOs explore energy-efficient consensus mechanisms and environmentally friendly approaches to blockchain technology. The goal is to minimize the ecological footprint of decentralized governance, ensuring that the growth of the ecosystem aligns with principles of environmental responsibility.

Interoperability and Ecosystem Integration

Interconnected DAO Ecosystems: The future of ICP DAOs envisions interconnected ecosystems, where multiple DAOs seamlessly interact and collaborate. Interoperability allows DAOs to share resources, leverage each other's strengths, and create a network effect that benefits the entire ecosystem. This interconnectedness fosters a dynamic environment where DAOs collectively contribute to the growth and innovation of the broader ICP ecosystem.

Cross-DAO Collaboration and Resource Sharing: ICP DAOs explore cross-DAO collaboration mechanisms that enable resource sharing and collaborative initiatives. From sharing research and development efforts to jointly funding projects, these collaborative models leverage the strengths of individual DAOs to create a synergistic effect. Inter-DAO resource sharing contributes to scalability by preventing duplication of efforts and optimizing the use of resources.

Challenges and Considerations in Scalability and Sustainability

Balancing Growth with Network Resilience: One of the challenges in the scalability of ICP DAOs is balancing growth with network resilience. As the ecosystem expands, the network must remain robust and resistant to potential attacks or disruptions. Decentralized decision-making becomes critical in addressing this challenge, ensuring that scaling decisions are made collectively and with a focus on preserving the integrity of the network.

User Experience and Accessibility: Scalability must be accompanied by a seamless user experience and accessibility. ICP DAOs need to prioritize user-friendly interfaces, efficient onboarding processes, and educational resources to cater to a diverse audience. Ensuring that scalability measures do not compromise user experience is essential for widespread adoption and sustained growth.

Real-world Impact: Empowering a Growing Ecosystem

Decentralized Governance at Scale: The scalability and sustainability strategies employed by ICP DAOs contribute to the real-world impact of decentralized governance at scale. The ability to accommodate a growing number of participants, handle increased transaction volume, and maintain network resilience positions ICP DAOs as effective tools for democratizing decision-making on a global scale.

Fostering Innovation and Collaboration: The interconnected and scalable nature of ICP DAOs fosters innovation and collaboration within the ecosystem. DAOs become hubs for creative solutions, collaborative projects, and iterative improvements. The real-world impact extends beyond individual DAOs, contributing to the collective innovation and growth of the broader ICP ecosystem.

Conclusion: Scaling Responsibly into a Sustainable Future

In the pursuit of scalability and sustainability, ICP DAOs chart a course into a future where decentralized governance is not only scalable but also aligned with principles of security, decentralization, and community empowerment. As we explore the impact of these strategies in the real world, subsequent chapters will unveil further dimensions of ICP DAOs, examining their role in addressing legal and regulatory considerations, and delving into their potential as tools for inclusive governance at the individual and community levels.

Interoperability and Ecosystem Integration: Connecting ICP DAOs to the Wider Blockchain Landscape

In envisioning the future trajectory of decentralized autonomous organizations (DAOs) within the Internet Computer Protocol (ICP) ecosystem, a critical dimension comes to the forefront—interoperability and ecosystem integration. This section explores the significance of connecting ICP DAOs to the wider blockchain landscape, fostering interoperability, and creating a collaborative environment that transcends individual ecosystems.

The Imperative of Interoperability

Defining Interoperability in Blockchain: Interoperability in the context of blockchain refers to the ability of different blockchain networks to communicate, share data, and execute transactions seamlessly. For ICP DAOs, interoperability is a strategic imperative as it enables them to transcend the confines of their own ecosystem, tap into external resources, and contribute to a more interconnected and collaborative blockchain landscape.

The Multichain Future: The blockchain space is evolving towards a multichain future, where various blockchain networks coexist and collaborate. ICP DAOs play a pivotal role in this landscape by embracing interoperability protocols, allowing them to communicate and transact with other blockchain networks. The vision is to create a decentralized internet of blockchains, where data and value can flow seamlessly across different ecosystems.

ICP DAOs and Cross-Chain Collaboration

Decentralized Finance (DeFi) Interoperability: One of the prominent areas where ICP DAOs explore interoperability is in the realm of decentralized finance (DeFi). By connecting with other blockchain networks hosting DeFi protocols, ICP DAOs can offer users a broader range of financial services, liquidity pools, and investment opportunities. Interoperability in DeFi fosters a more inclusive and diverse financial ecosystem.

Cross-Chain Asset Transfers: Interoperability facilitates cross-chain asset transfers, enabling assets to move seamlessly between ICP DAOs and other blockchain networks. This capability opens up new possibilities for decentralized exchanges, liquidity providers, and asset managers, allowing them to tap into a global pool of assets and liquidity. Cross-chain asset transfers contribute to a more efficient and interconnected decentralized financial infrastructure.

Interoperability Protocols in the ICP Ecosystem

Canister Smart Contracts and Cross-Chain Communication: ICP DAOs leverage the inherent capabilities of canister smart contracts to enable cross-chain communication. These smart contracts act as bridges between the ICP ecosystem and other blockchains, facilitating the transfer of data and assets. Canister smart contracts play a foundational role in building interoperability bridges, ensuring that ICP DAOs can seamlessly interact with a diverse array of blockchain networks.

Standardization and Interoperability Standards: Standardization of interoperability protocols becomes essential for creating a cohesive and efficient multichain ecosystem. ICP DAOs actively participate in the development and adoption of interoperability standards that ensure compatibility with other blockchain networks. These standards cover areas such as cross-chain messaging, asset representation, and consensus mechanisms, laying the groundwork for seamless interoperability.

Cross-Protocol Collaboration and Ecosystem Integration

Connecting with Ethereum and Other Blockchains: ICP DAOs seek to connect with established blockchain networks, including Ethereum, to tap into existing ecosystems, user bases, and decentralized applications

(DApps). Bridging ICP DAOs with Ethereum opens up new possibilities for cross-protocol collaboration, allowing users and developers to leverage the strengths of both ecosystems. This interoperability fosters a collaborative environment where innovation can thrive across blockchain networks.

Decentralized Application Portability: Interoperability enables decentralized application (DApp) portability, allowing developers to build applications that can run seamlessly on multiple blockchains. ICP DAOs embrace this approach, supporting the development of DApps that can transcend the boundaries of the ICP ecosystem and operate on other compatible blockchains. DApp portability contributes to a more fluid and interconnected decentralized application landscape.

Challenges and Considerations in Interoperability

Security and Trust in Cross-Chain Transactions: Interoperability introduces challenges related to security and trust in cross-chain transactions. ICP DAOs must address issues such as double-spending, consensus mechanisms misalignment, and potential vulnerabilities in the communication between different blockchains. Implementing robust security measures and adopting trusted interoperability standards are essential to mitigate these challenges and build confidence in cross-chain transactions.

Regulatory Compliance in Multichain Environments: As ICP DAOs engage in cross-chain transactions and collaboration, regulatory compliance becomes a complex consideration. Different blockchains may be subject to varying regulatory frameworks, requiring ICP DAOs to navigate a diverse landscape of legal requirements. Collaborative efforts within the blockchain community, engagement with regulatory bodies, and the development of interoperability standards that align with regulatory expectations are crucial for ensuring compliance.

Real-world Impact: Fostering a Multichain Ecosystem

Global Access to Decentralized Services: Interoperability in ICP DAOs translates to global access to decentralized services. Users and developers can engage with a diverse range of blockchain networks, accessing decentralized applications, financial services, and assets seamlessly. This global accessibility fosters inclusivity and democratizes access to decentralized technologies, irrespective of geographic boundaries.

Cross-Chain Collaboration for Innovation: The collaboration between ICP DAOs and other blockchain networks catalyzes innovation. Developers and entrepreneurs can leverage the strengths of different ecosystems, combining resources, expertise, and user bases. Cross-chain collaboration becomes a driving force for innovation, leading to the development of novel solutions, interoperable applications, and a more vibrant decentralized technology landscape.

Conclusion: Building Bridges to a Multichain Future

In connecting ICP DAOs to the wider blockchain landscape, the vision is not just about interoperability but about building bridges to a multichain future. ICP DAOs, through their commitment to interoperability standards and cross-protocol collaboration, contribute to the evolution of a decentralized internet of blockchains. As we explore the impact of these efforts, subsequent chapters will unveil further dimensions of ICP DAOs, addressing legal and regulatory considerations, and delving into their potential as tools for inclusive governance at the individual and community levels.

Empowering Individuals and Communities: ICP DAOs as a Tool for Inclusive Governance

In the unfolding narrative of decentralized autonomous organizations (DAOs) within the Internet Computer Protocol (ICP) ecosystem, a profound vision emerges—one of empowerment for individuals and communities. This section delves into the transformative potential of ICP DAOs as instruments for inclusive governance, exploring their role in democratizing decision-making, fostering community participation, and empowering diverse voices within the decentralized landscape.

Democratizing Decision-Making Through DAOs

Foundations of Inclusive Governance: At the heart of ICP DAOs lies the foundational principle of inclusive governance. Inclusive governance entails a departure from traditional models, where decision-making power is concentrated in a few entities, to a more democratic and participatory approach. ICP DAOs leverage decentralized technologies to ensure that individuals, regardless of their background or geographical location, have a voice in the decision-making processes that shape the trajectory of the organization.

Participatory Decision-Making: ICP DAOs facilitate participatory decision-making, allowing community members to actively contribute to discussions, propose initiatives, and vote on important matters. The decentralized nature of decision-making processes ensures that decisions are not imposed from a central authority but arise from the collective wisdom and consensus of the community. This participatory model fosters a sense of ownership and responsibility among community members.

Community Incentives and Tokenomics

Aligning Interests Through Tokenomics: Tokenomics plays a pivotal role in aligning the interests of individuals with the success of ICP DAOs. By distributing governance tokens to participants based on their contributions, DAOs create a system where active engagement is rewarded. Governance tokens represent not only a form of ownership within the DAO but also a stake in the decision-making processes. This alignment of interests through tokenomics incentivizes sustained participation and commitment from the community.

Inclusive Distribution Models: ICP DAOs explore inclusive distribution models that ensure a broad and diverse representation within the community. By avoiding concentrations of governance tokens in the hands of a few, DAOs aim to prevent the centralization of power and decision-making influence. Inclusive distribution models may include airdrops, community grants, or other mechanisms that prioritize accessibility and diversity in token ownership.

Decentralized Identity and Accessibility

Ensuring Inclusive Access: Inclusive governance in ICP DAOs goes beyond tokenomics to encompass decentralized identity and accessibility. The goal is to ensure that individuals from diverse backgrounds, including those who may not have traditional access to financial systems, can participate in DAO activities. Decentralized identity systems provide a mechanism for individuals to establish their digital identity in a secure and verifiable manner, opening the doors to wider participation.

Accessibility and User-Friendly Interfaces: User-friendly interfaces and accessible platforms are integral to inclusive governance. ICP DAOs prioritize the development of interfaces that are intuitive, easy to navigate, and cater to users with varying levels of technical expertise. The goal is to democratize access to decentralized technologies, making participation in governance processes accessible to a broader audience.

Cultural and Linguistic Diversity

Embracing Cultural Diversity: ICP DAOs recognize the importance of cultural diversity in fostering inclusive governance. Cultural perspectives influence decision-making, and DAOs strive to create environments where individuals from different cultural backgrounds feel represented and heard. Initiatives that celebrate cultural diversity, language inclusivity, and global representation contribute to the richness of the decentralized governance experience.

Linguistic Inclusivity: In the pursuit of inclusivity, ICP DAOs acknowledge the role of language as a potential barrier to participation. Efforts are made to provide information, conduct discussions, and disseminate governance-related content in multiple languages. Multilingual support ensures that individuals from diverse linguistic backgrounds can engage meaningfully in the decision-making processes of the DAO.

Community-Driven Initiatives and Impact

Community-Led Governance Proposals: ICP DAOs empower community members to initiate governance proposals that align with the values and goals of the community. These proposals can range from protocol upgrades to community initiatives, reflecting the diverse interests and priorities within the DAO. Community-led governance ensures that decisions are responsive to the evolving needs and aspirations of the community.

Impact on Local and Global Communities: The impact of ICP DAOs extends beyond their immediate community to influence local and global initiatives. DAOs engage in social impact projects, environmental sustainability efforts, and community-driven initiatives that contribute to the greater good. The decentralized and borderless nature of DAOs enables them to catalyze positive change on a global scale, empowering communities to address challenges and seize opportunities.

Challenges and Considerations in Inclusive Governance

Ensuring Diversity of Participation: While inclusive governance is a guiding principle, ensuring the diversity of participation remains a ongoing challenge. DAOs actively address barriers to entry, such as technical complexity, by providing educational resources and support. Strategies to encourage underrepresented groups to participate, including outreach programs and mentorship initiatives, are essential to achieving a truly inclusive governance landscape.

Balancing Inclusivity and Efficiency: Striking the right balance between inclusivity and efficiency is a nuanced consideration. As DAOs grow, the challenge lies in managing decision-making processes to accommodate a larger and more diverse community while maintaining the agility and effectiveness of governance. DAOs experiment with governance models, voting mechanisms, and decision-making frameworks to find the optimal balance.

Real-world Impact: Inclusion as a Catalyst for Change

Empowering Marginalized Communities: Inclusive governance through ICP DAOs becomes a catalyst for empowering marginalized communities. By providing a platform for individuals who may have been excluded from traditional decision-making structures, DAOs amplify diverse voices and perspectives. The empowerment of marginalized communities extends to economic opportunities, access to resources, and active participation in shaping their collective future.

Addressing Global Challenges: ICP DAOs leverage inclusive governance to address global challenges. From climate initiatives to humanitarian projects, DAOs become vehicles for community-led solutions to pressing issues. The decentralized and collaborative nature of governance in ICP DAOs positions them as agile and responsive entities that can adapt to the changing needs of the world.

Conclusion: Redefining Governance through Inclusivity

In the vision for the future of ICP DAOs, inclusivity becomes a defining feature of decentralized governance. By empowering individuals and communities, democratizing decision-making, and fostering diversity, ICP DAOs reshape the landscape of governance. As we explore the impact of inclusive governance, subsequent chapters will unveil further dimensions of ICP DAOs, addressing legal and regulatory considerations, and delving into the practicalities of designing, implementing, and assessing the performance of ICP DAOs.

Chapter 5: Legal and Regulatory Considerations for ICP DAOs

Navigating the Legal Landscape: Understanding the Regulatory Framework for ICP DAOs

In the rapidly evolving landscape of decentralized autonomous organizations (DAOs) within the Internet Computer Protocol (ICP) ecosystem, navigating the legal terrain is a critical aspect of ensuring sustainable growth and widespread adoption. This section delves into the complexities of the legal and regulatory considerations for ICP DAOs, providing insights into understanding the regulatory framework, compliance challenges, and strategies for navigating the legal landscape.

The Regulatory Tapestry of Decentralized Governance

Defining the Regulatory Landscape: ICP DAOs operate within a multifaceted regulatory landscape that spans national, regional, and international jurisdictions. Understanding this regulatory tapestry is essential for DAOs to ensure compliance and mitigate legal risks. The decentralized nature of DAOs introduces unique challenges as traditional legal frameworks may not seamlessly align with the novel aspects of decentralized governance.

Regulatory Clarity and Uncertainty: One of the primary challenges for ICP DAOs is the current lack of regulatory clarity. The decentralized nature of these organizations often falls outside traditional regulatory categories, leaving legal frameworks struggling to catch up with the pace of innovation. The resulting uncertainty poses challenges for DAOs seeking to operate within the bounds of the law while pushing the boundaries of decentralized governance.

Decentralization and Regulatory Challenges

Decentralization as a Legal Paradigm: Decentralization, a cornerstone of DAOs, introduces a paradigm shift in how legal frameworks traditionally view organizations. Unlike centralized entities with identifiable legal structures, DAOs are often decentralized networks of participants making collective decisions. This departure from conventional organizational structures raises questions about legal liability, accountability, and the application of existing regulatory frameworks.

Regulatory Challenges in Decentralized Decision-Making: Decentralized decision-making, a core feature of DAOs, challenges traditional notions of hierarchical authority. Legal frameworks that rely on clear lines of responsibility and accountability face challenges in adapting to the distributed and consensus-driven decision-making processes inherent in DAOs. Navigating these challenges requires a nuanced understanding of both decentralized governance principles and existing regulatory expectations.

Jurisdictional Variances in Regulatory Approaches

National and International Variances: ICP DAOs operate in a global context, transcending national borders and jurisdictions. This global reach introduces a complex interplay of regulatory approaches, with different countries adopting varied stances on the legal status of DAOs. While some jurisdictions embrace innovation and provide regulatory sandboxes for experimentation, others may approach decentralized governance with caution or skepticism.

Harmonizing International Standards: The need for harmonizing international standards for DAOs becomes evident as these organizations seek to operate globally. Efforts to establish common ground and shared principles at the international level can facilitate a more coherent regulatory framework. Organizations, industry associations, and regulatory bodies play a pivotal role in advocating for standardized approaches that balance innovation with regulatory responsibility.

Understanding Regulatory Classifications for DAOs

DAOs as Legal Entities: The legal classification of DAOs as entities poses a fundamental challenge. Traditional legal structures recognize entities with defined legal personalities, such as corporations or partnerships. DAOs, by contrast, lack a central governing authority, raising questions about their legal identity. Some jurisdictions explore innovative legal structures, such as the creation of decentralized autonomous associations, to accommodate the unique nature of DAOs.

Token Classification and Regulatory Impact: Tokens, often integral to DAOs as a means of participation and governance, face diverse regulatory classifications. Depending on their characteristics, tokens may be categorized as securities, commodities, or utilities, each subject to different regulatory regimes. Understanding the implications of token classifications is crucial for DAOs to navigate regulatory requirements and ensure compliance.

Compliance Strategies for ICP DAOs

Engaging in Regulatory Dialogue: Proactive engagement with regulatory bodies is a strategic approach for ICP DAOs navigating the legal landscape. Establishing a dialogue with regulators provides an opportunity to educate authorities about the decentralized nature of DAOs, address concerns, and contribute to the development of regulatory frameworks that foster innovation while ensuring consumer protection and legal compliance.

Developing Self-Regulatory Mechanisms: In the absence of clear regulatory guidance, DAOs may consider developing self-regulatory mechanisms. This includes establishing governance structures that prioritize transparency, accountability, and compliance with legal standards. Codes of conduct, audits, and voluntary compliance measures can demonstrate a commitment to responsible governance and build trust with both participants and regulatory authorities.

Challenges in Legal Compliance for ICP DAOs

Contractual Governance and Legal Enforceability: The contractual nature of governance in DAOs raises questions about the legal enforceability of smart contracts and decentralized decisions. While smart contracts are designed to execute autonomously based on predefined rules, the legal standing of these contracts in traditional legal systems may be uncertain. Establishing mechanisms for legal recognition and enforceability is an ongoing challenge for DAOs.

Cross-Border Legal Risks: Operating in a global context exposes DAOs to cross-border legal risks. Variances in regulatory approaches, legal interpretations, and enforcement mechanisms across jurisdictions can create a complex landscape for DAOs. Mitigating cross-border legal risks involves comprehensive legal analysis, collaboration with legal experts in different jurisdictions, and strategic decision-making to navigate diverse regulatory environments.

Real-world Impact: Navigating the Legal Frontier

Legal Compliance as a Catalyst for Adoption: Navigating the legal frontier is not only a compliance necessity but also a catalyst for adoption. ICP DAOs that demonstrate a commitment to legal compliance enhance their credibility and attract a broader community of participants. Clear legal frameworks provide reassurance to users, developers, and investors, fostering an environment where DAOs can thrive and contribute to the broader decentralized ecosystem.

Legal Innovation and Regulatory Evolution: ICP DAOs contribute to legal innovation by challenging existing frameworks and catalyzing regulatory evolution. As regulators grapple with the complexities of decentralized governance, the dialogue between DAOs and regulatory bodies becomes a driving force for regulatory adaptation. This dynamic interaction shapes the legal landscape for DAOs and sets precedents for future regulatory approaches to decentralized technologies.

Conclusion: Charting a Course through Legal Uncertainty

In navigating the legal landscape, ICP DAOs chart a course through uncertainty, innovation, and regulatory evolution. The decentralized nature of DAOs challenges traditional legal paradigms, necessitating a collaborative and proactive approach to legal compliance. As we delve further into legal and regulatory considerations, subsequent chapters will explore intellectual property rights, taxation implications, data privacy, and provide a practical guide for the design, implementation, and assessment of ICP DAOs within the legal framework.

Intellectual Property Rights (IPR) and ICP DAOs: Protecting Innovation in the Digital Age

In the dynamic landscape of decentralized autonomous organizations (DAOs) within the Internet Computer Protocol (ICP) ecosystem, the intersection of innovation and intellectual property rights (IPR) poses intricate challenges and opportunities. This section explores the evolving landscape of IPR within the realm of ICP DAOs, shedding light on the protection of innovative endeavors, collaboration dynamics, and the broader implications for intellectual property in the digital age.

The Nature of Innovation in ICP DAOs

Decentralized Innovation Ecosystem: ICP DAOs serve as incubators of innovation, fostering a decentralized ecosystem where contributors collaboratively develop and implement novel solutions. From protocol upgrades to the creation of decentralized applications (DApps), innovation is inherent in the DNA of DAOs. The challenge lies in navigating the nuances of IPR within the decentralized paradigm, where traditional concepts of ownership and intellectual property face transformation.

Smart Contracts and Code as Creative Expression: Smart contracts, the building blocks of ICP DAOs, are not just lines of code but manifestations of creative expression.

In the digital age, code is a form of intellectual creation that drives the functionality and governance of DAOs. The protection of smart contracts as intellectual property involves grappling with the unique nature of code as a dynamic and collaborative creation shaped by multiple contributors.

Decentralized Collaboration and IPR Challenges

Collaborative Code Development: ICP DAOs thrive on collaborative code development, where contributors from diverse backgrounds participate in shaping the protocols and applications. The decentralized and open nature of collaboration introduces challenges to traditional IPR models, which often rely on clear ownership and delineation of contributions. Navigating the intricacies of collaborative code development requires a nuanced approach to IPR within DAOs.

Code Attribution and Ownership: Determining code attribution and ownership in decentralized collaboration is a complex endeavor. Traditional intellectual property models, such as copyright law, may struggle to accommodate the fluid and distributed nature of code contributions within DAOs. Clear and transparent governance structures, alongside innovative approaches to code attribution, become essential for addressing issues of ownership and recognition.

IPR Considerations for Smart Contracts and Protocols

Smart Contracts as Copyrightable Works: The question of whether smart contracts qualify as copyrightable works introduces a nuanced dimension to IPR considerations. While code is generally considered eligible for copyright protection, the decentralized and collaborative nature of smart contract development raises questions about individual authorship and the collective nature of code creation within DAOs. Balancing individual contributors' rights with the collective ownership of DAOs becomes a focal point.

Open Source and Licensing Strategies: Many ICP DAOs embrace open-source principles, making their code publicly accessible and inviting contributions from the broader community. Open-source licensing strategies play a crucial role in shaping the IPR landscape for DAOs. Choosing the right license, whether permissive or copyleft, influences how contributors can use, modify, and distribute the code. The selection of licensing models reflects the DAO's values and its approach to fostering collaboration while protecting innovation.

Tokenomics, DAO Treasuries, and IPR Protection

Tokenomics and Incentivizing Innovation: Tokenomics, the economic model underlying ICP DAOs, introduces incentives for innovation through token rewards. Contributors are often rewarded with governance tokens or other crypto-assets for their contributions. The integration of tokenomics with IPR protection involves aligning these incentives with mechanisms that recognize and reward creative contributions, fostering a symbiotic relationship between token holders and innovators.

DAO Treasuries and Funding Innovation: DAO treasuries, comprising funds collected through token sales or other mechanisms, serve as a critical resource for funding innovation. Protecting the IPR associated with innovations funded by DAO treasuries requires careful consideration of ownership, licensing, and governance structures. Ensuring that DAOs can continue to invest in and benefit from the intellectual property they fund becomes integral to sustaining innovation.

IPR Challenges in Cross-Protocol Collaboration

Cross-Protocol Collaboration Dynamics: ICP DAOs often engage in cross-protocol collaboration, where different DAOs contribute to shared initiatives or collaborate on interoperable solutions. This collaboration introduces IPR challenges related to the integration of codebases, the use of shared resources, and the potential for conflicts in intellectual property ownership. Establishing clear frameworks for collaboration and addressing IPR considerations in cross-protocol initiatives becomes crucial.

Conflict Resolution Mechanisms: In the decentralized landscape, conflict resolution mechanisms for IPR disputes require innovative approaches. Traditional legal avenues may be ill-suited to address disputes arising from decentralized collaboration. DAOs explore decentralized arbitration, governance-based conflict resolution, or other consensus-driven mechanisms to resolve IPR conflicts. These mechanisms aim to strike a balance between protecting intellectual property and fostering collaborative innovation.

Open Innovation and the Commons

Embracing Open Innovation Principles: ICP DAOs often embrace open innovation principles, fostering a culture of transparency, collaboration, and shared knowledge. Open innovation challenges traditional notions of proprietary ownership, emphasizing the collective advancement of knowledge and technology. DAOs act as catalysts for open innovation, contributing to the commons and promoting the idea that shared intellectual resources can drive broader societal benefits.

Building the Intellectual Commons: DAOs contribute to building the intellectual commons, a shared repository of knowledge and code that transcends individual ownership. The concept of the commons challenges conventional IPR models, envisioning a landscape where innovations are freely accessible for the benefit of all. DAOs play a pivotal role in defining the boundaries, governance, and sustainability of the intellectual commons within the decentralized ecosystem.

Real-world Impact: Fostering a Culture of Innovation

Empowering Creators and Contributors: In navigating the complexities of IPR, ICP DAOs empower creators and contributors by recognizing and rewarding their innovative efforts. Tokenomics, DAO treasuries, and collaborative governance structures create a culture where individuals are incentivized to contribute, knowing that their intellectual contributions are valued and protected. This empowerment extends to a diverse community of developers, designers, and thinkers who shape the trajectory of decentralized innovation.

Sustaining Long-term Innovation: The IPR considerations within ICP DAOs contribute to sustaining long-term innovation. By establishing clear frameworks for code attribution, ownership, and collaboration, DAOs create environments conducive to ongoing contributions and advancements. The interplay between IPR protection, open innovation principles, and decentralized collaboration positions ICP DAOs as engines of sustained innovation in the digital age.

Conclusion: Redefining IPR in the Decentralized Paradigm

In navigating the realm of intellectual property rights, ICP DAOs redefine the traditional paradigms of ownership and innovation. The collaborative and decentralized nature of these organizations challenges existing IPR models, inviting a reevaluation of how intellectual contributions are recognized, protected, and shared. As we delve further into legal and regulatory considerations, subsequent chapters will explore taxation implications, data privacy, and provide a practical guide for the design, implementation, and assessment of ICP DAOs within the legal framework.

Taxation and Financial Compliance: Navigating Tax Implications for ICP DAOs

In the decentralized landscape of Internet Computer Protocol (ICP) DAOs, taxation and financial compliance emerge as critical considerations. This section delves into the complex terrain of tax implications for ICP DAOs, exploring the challenges posed by decentralized governance structures, tokenomics, and the evolving landscape of taxation in the digital realm.

Decentralized Governance Structures and Tax Complexity

Decentralization and Tax Jurisdiction Challenges: The decentralized nature of ICP DAOs introduces unique challenges in determining tax jurisdictions. Traditional tax frameworks are often designed for centralized entities with clear legal structures, making it challenging to apply existing regulations to DAOs. The fluid and borderless nature of decentralized governance structures complicates the assessment of where tax obligations arise, raising questions about how different jurisdictions will treat DAO activities.

Tax Classification of DAOs: The classification of DAOs for tax purposes remains a gray area in many jurisdictions. DAOs, lacking traditional legal personalities, may be treated differently based on the tax classification chosen by regulatory bodies. The choice between viewing DAOs as associations, partnerships, or other legal entities significantly impacts the tax obligations and liabilities for both the DAO itself and its participants.

Tokenomics, Revenue Streams, and Tax Liabilities

Tokenomics and Taxation: The tokenomics of ICP DAOs, including the issuance and distribution of governance tokens, impact the tax landscape for both the DAO and its participants. Understanding how tokens are classified for tax purposes—whether as securities, commodities, or utilities—determines the applicable tax treatment. The intricacies of tokenomics, including airdrops, staking rewards, and token sales, contribute to the complexity of assessing tax liabilities.

Revenue Streams and Taxable Events: ICP DAOs engage in various activities that generate revenue, including token sales, transaction fees, and fundraising through DAO treasuries. Each of these activities may trigger taxable events with implications for the DAO's financial compliance. Navigating the classification of revenue streams and understanding the tax consequences of each activity become essential aspects of ensuring compliance with tax regulations.

Tax Treatment of DAO Participants

Tax Obligations for Contributors: Individuals contributing to ICP DAOs face their own set of tax obligations. Receipt of governance tokens, participation in staking, and other activities within the DAO may lead to tax liabilities for contributors. Determining the fair market value of tokens received and understanding the tax implications of different forms of compensation are integral to ensuring that contributors fulfill their tax obligations.

Staking and Yield Farming Tax Considerations: Staking and yield farming, common activities within ICP DAOs, introduce specific tax considerations. The rewards generated from staking and yield farming may be subject to income tax, capital gains tax, or other relevant tax categories. Participants engaging in these activities must navigate the tax landscape to accurately report and comply with tax obligations associated with their staking and yield farming activities.

Cross-Border Taxation Challenges

Cross-Border Activities and Tax Reporting: ICP DAOs operate in a global context, with contributors and participants spanning multiple jurisdictions. Cross-border activities introduce complexities in tax reporting, compliance, and withholding obligations. The lack of standardized international tax regulations for DAOs exacerbates the challenges, requiring a nuanced understanding of the tax implications associated with decentralized collaboration on a global scale.

Withholding Tax and Cross-Border Transactions: Cross-border transactions within ICP DAOs may trigger withholding tax obligations, particularly when funds move across borders or contributors from different jurisdictions receive rewards. Determining the applicability of withholding tax, understanding the rates, and complying with reporting requirements become crucial aspects of financial compliance for DAOs engaged in international activities.

Financial Compliance Strategies for ICP DAOs

Transparent Financial Reporting: Transparent financial reporting is a cornerstone of financial compliance for ICP DAOs. Establishing clear and auditable records of financial transactions, revenue streams, and token distributions ensures accountability and facilitates compliance with tax regulations. Transparent reporting not only fulfills regulatory requirements but also builds trust with participants, contributors, and regulatory bodies.

Collaboration with Tax Professionals: Given the complex and evolving nature of tax regulations for decentralized entities, collaboration with tax professionals becomes imperative. Tax experts with knowledge of both traditional financial systems and the intricacies of decentralized finance can provide valuable insights. DAOs should engage with tax professionals to navigate the nuances of tax regulations, assess risks, and develop compliant financial strategies.

Regulatory Guidance and Advocacy

Engaging with Regulators: ICP DAOs can proactively engage with regulators to seek clarity on tax regulations and advocate for frameworks that accommodate the unique aspects of decentralized governance. Regulatory dialogue becomes a strategic approach to foster understanding, address uncertainties, and contribute to the development of tax frameworks that support innovation within the decentralized ecosystem.

Industry Advocacy and Best Practices: Industry advocacy and the development of best practices play a crucial role in shaping regulatory frameworks. DAOs, industry associations, and stakeholders can collaborate to establish standards for financial compliance, tax reporting, and governance. Advocacy efforts contribute to the creation of regulatory environments that foster innovation while ensuring responsible financial practices.

Real-world Impact: Compliance as a Catalyst for Growth

Building Credibility and Trust: Compliance with tax regulations and financial reporting requirements is not merely a legal obligation but a catalyst for building credibility and trust. ICP DAOs that demonstrate a commitment to financial compliance enhance their reputation, attract a broader community of participants, and create an environment conducive to sustained growth.

Sustainable Financial Strategies: Navigating tax implications and financial compliance contributes to the development of sustainable financial strategies for ICP DAOs. By understanding the tax landscape, managing liabilities, and implementing transparent financial practices, DAOs position themselves for long-term success. Sustainable financial strategies not only ensure regulatory compliance but also support ongoing innovation and community engagement.

Conclusion: Navigating the Evolving Tax Landscape

In navigating the evolving tax landscape, ICP DAOs embark on a journey to balance innovation with financial responsibility. The challenges presented by decentralized governance structures, tokenomics, and cross-border activities necessitate a proactive and collaborative approach to financial compliance. As we explore further legal and regulatory considerations, subsequent chapters will delve into data privacy, offering a practical guide for the design, implementation, and assessment of ICP DAOs within the legal and financial framework.

Data Privacy and Security: Protecting User Data in the ICP DAO Ecosystem

In the era of decentralized autonomous organizations (DAOs) within the Internet Computer Protocol (ICP) ecosystem, data privacy and security emerge as paramount concerns. This section delves into the complex landscape of safeguarding user data within ICP DAOs, exploring the challenges presented by decentralized governance, the role of smart contracts, and the evolving regulatory frameworks shaping data protection.

Decentralized Governance and User Data

Decentralization and User Data Ownership: The decentralized governance model inherent in ICP DAOs introduces a paradigm shift in how user data ownership is conceptualized. Unlike traditional centralized platforms, where user data is typically owned and controlled by the platform itself, DAOs empower users by allowing them to retain ownership of their data. Decentralization fosters a more equitable relationship between users and DAOs, aligning with the principles of data autonomy and user empowerment.

Challenges of User Data Fragmentation: While decentralized governance grants users greater control over their data, it also introduces challenges related to data fragmentation. User data may be distributed across various smart contracts, canisters, or subnets within the ICP DAO ecosystem. Managing and securing fragmented user data while preserving user sovereignty becomes a complex task, necessitating innovative solutions for data interoperability and privacy.

Smart Contracts and Data Security

Smart Contracts as Custodians of Data: Smart contracts play a pivotal role in ICP DAOs, acting as custodians of user data and facilitating decentralized decision-making. The transparent and auditable nature of smart contracts enhances data security by providing visibility into how user data is accessed, processed, and utilized within the DAO. However, ensuring the secure execution of smart contracts and protecting against vulnerabilities becomes imperative to maintain user trust.

Code Audits and Security Assessments: Conducting regular code audits and security assessments of smart contracts is a foundational practice for data security within ICP DAOs. These assessments involve scrutinizing the codebase for potential vulnerabilities, ensuring compliance with security best practices, and identifying any potential risks that could compromise user data. Rigorous security measures contribute to building a robust foundation for protecting sensitive information.

Privacy by Design in Decentralized Systems

Privacy by Design Principles: Privacy by design, a foundational concept in data protection, becomes even more critical in decentralized systems like ICP DAOs. Implementing privacy by design involves embedding data protection measures into the architecture and governance processes from the outset. By incorporating privacy considerations into the design of smart contracts, canisters, and governance structures, DAOs can proactively mitigate privacy risks and enhance user data protection.

Decentralized Identity Solutions: Decentralized identity solutions, such as self-sovereign identity (SSI), contribute to privacy by design within ICP DAOs. These solutions empower users with control over their identity information, allowing them to selectively disclose data as needed. Implementing decentralized identity mitigates the risks associated with centralized identity management systems and aligns with the principles of user-centric data control.

Regulatory Frameworks for Data Protection

Evolution of Data Protection Laws: The evolving landscape of data protection laws globally, such as the

General Data Protection Regulation (GDPR) in the European Union, underscores the importance of regulatory compliance for ICP DAOs. While decentralized systems challenge traditional notions of data controllership, DAOs must navigate the regulatory framework to ensure alignment with user privacy rights and avoid legal consequences.

Extraterritorial Reach of Data Regulations: Data protection laws often extend beyond national borders, impacting DAOs that operate on a global scale. The extraterritorial reach of regulations requires DAOs to consider the implications of diverse data protection laws, even if the DAO itself doesn't have a physical presence in certain jurisdictions. Harmonizing data protection practices to meet the highest standard ensures compliance with various regulatory regimes.

User Consent and Transparent Data Practices

Informed Consent in DAO Interactions: In a decentralized context, obtaining informed consent from users takes on heightened significance. DAOs must communicate transparently about how user data will be used, processed, and shared within the ecosystem. Implementing mechanisms for users to provide explicit consent aligns with privacy principles and fosters a relationship of trust between the DAO and its community.

Transparent Data Practices: Transparency in data practices involves providing users with clear information about how their data is handled within the DAO ecosystem. This includes detailing data processing activities, specifying the purposes for which data is collected, and elucidating any third-party involvement. Transparent data practices not only facilitate compliance with regulations but also contribute to building a culture of openness within the decentralized community.

Security Breach Response and Incident Management

Proactive Security Measures: While prevention is crucial, recognizing the inevitability of potential security breaches is equally important. DAOs should implement proactive security measures, including encryption protocols, access controls, and regular security audits, to minimize the risk of unauthorized access and data breaches. These measures bolster the DAO's resilience against external threats.

Incident Response Plans: Developing robust incident response plans is a fundamental aspect of data security within ICP DAOs. In the event of a security breach, having a well-defined plan ensures a swift and coordinated response to mitigate the impact on user data. Incident response plans typically include communication strategies, legal considerations, and steps to remediate vulnerabilities and prevent future incidents.

Community Education and Empowerment

Educating Users on Data Privacy: Empowering users with knowledge about data privacy and security is a shared responsibility between DAOs and their communities. DAOs should invest in educational initiatives to inform users about the importance of data privacy, their rights, and the measures implemented to protect their data. Community education builds a collective awareness of data protection principles and fosters a sense of ownership over personal information.

Community Involvement in Governance: Involving the community in governance decisions related to data privacy enhances transparency and ensures that user perspectives are considered. DAOs can integrate community feedback into the development of privacy policies, security measures, and governance structures related to user data. Community participation fosters a sense of co-ownership in the protection of data within the decentralized ecosystem.

Real-world Impact: Fostering Trust in the Decentralized Community

Building Trust through Data Protection: In a decentralized landscape where user empowerment is paramount, fostering trust through robust data protection practices is a cornerstone of success. ICP DAOs that prioritize user privacy, implement security measures, and engage in transparent communication build a foundation of trust that contributes to the sustained growth of the decentralized community.

Contributing to Privacy Standards: ICP DAOs play a pioneering role in contributing to privacy standards within the decentralized space. By implementing innovative solutions, adhering to best practices, and actively engaging with regulatory bodies, DAOs contribute to the establishment of privacy standards that safeguard user data and elevate the overall reputation of decentralized governance.

Conclusion: Pioneering Data Protection in Decentralized Governance

In navigating the intricate landscape of data privacy and security, ICP DAOs pioneer innovative solutions that redefine user data protection in decentralized governance. The challenges presented by decentralized governance structures, smart contracts, and evolving regulatory frameworks necessitate a proactive and collaborative approach to safeguarding user data. As we continue to explore legal and regulatory considerations, subsequent chapters will offer a practical guide for the design, implementation, and assessment of ICP DAOs within the legal, financial, and privacy framework.

Chapter 6: Realizing the Potential of ICP DAOs: A Practical Guide for Implementation

Designing and Implementing an ICP DAO: A Step-by-Step Approach

Embarking on the journey to design and implement an Internet Computer Protocol (ICP) Decentralized Autonomous Organization (DAO) requires a comprehensive and strategic approach. This step-by-step guide aims to provide practical insights and considerations for organizations, developers, and communities looking to leverage the transformative potential of ICP DAOs.

Understanding the Objectives and Scope

Before diving into the technicalities of DAO implementation, it's crucial to clearly define the objectives and scope of the DAO. Consider the purpose of the DAO, whether it's for governance, decentralized finance (DeFi), community initiatives, or a combination of these. Establish the scope by identifying the specific functions, decision-making processes, and areas of community involvement the DAO will encompass.

Selecting the Right Governance Model

Choosing an appropriate governance model is a foundational decision that shapes the entire functioning of the DAO. ICP DAOs often adopt models such as Token-based

Governance, Liquid Democracy, or Quadratic Voting. Evaluate the strengths and weaknesses of each model in the context of the DAO's objectives. Consider factors such as inclusivity, efficiency, and adaptability to make an informed decision.

Defining Tokenomics and Economic Incentives

Tokenomics, the economic model underlying the DAO, involves designing the distribution, utility, and incentives associated with the governance token. Define the tokenomics to align with the DAO's goals. Consider aspects such as token distribution mechanisms, utility within the ecosystem, and incentives for active participation. Striking a balance between rewarding contributors and ensuring long-term sustainability is key.

Selecting Smart Contract Platforms and Languages

ICP DAOs leverage smart contracts as the building blocks of their functionality. Choose the appropriate smart contract platform, and language based on factors such as security, scalability, and ease of development. The Motoko programming language, designed for the Internet Computer, is a popular choice. Ensure compatibility with the ICP ecosystem and consider the learning curve for developers involved in the implementation.

Building Governance Smart Contracts

Developing smart contracts that govern the DAO's operations is a critical step. This involves coding the logic for proposal creation, voting mechanisms, and the execution of decisions. Pay attention to security best practices, conduct thorough code audits, and ensure that the smart contracts are designed to evolve with the DAO's needs. Transparent and auditable code contributes to user trust.

Implementing a User-Friendly Interface

User experience is paramount in ensuring widespread adoption and engagement. Design an intuitive and user-friendly interface that allows community members to participate in DAO activities seamlessly. Consider features such as proposal submission, voting, and tracking governance token balances. Accessibility and simplicity are key elements to encourage active community involvement.

Integrating Identity and Reputation Systems

Implementing identity and reputation systems contributes to the accountability and authenticity of participants. Explore decentralized identity solutions, such as self-sovereign identity (SSI), to empower users with control over their identity information. Reputation systems can be leveraged to recognize and reward active contributors based on their past contributions to the DAO.

Addressing Security and Risk Management

Security is a top priority in DAO implementation. Implement robust security measures, conduct regular code audits, and stay informed about potential vulnerabilities. Consider establishing a bug bounty program to incentivize external security researchers to identify and report vulnerabilities. Develop and document a comprehensive risk management plan to address potential challenges and unforeseen issues.

Community Engagement and Onboarding Strategies

Community engagement is essential for the success of an ICP DAO. Develop strategies for onboarding new members and actively involving the community in decision-making processes. Leverage communication channels, social media, and community forums to foster discussions, gather feedback, and create a sense of belonging. Regularly update the community on DAO activities and achievements to maintain transparency.

Testing and Iterating the DAO Model

Prior to full deployment, conduct thorough testing of the DAO model in a controlled environment. Test the governance mechanisms, smart contracts, and user interfaces to identify and address any issues. Iterate based on feedback from the testing phase, ensuring that the DAO model is resilient, efficient, and aligns with the community's expectations. Implementing a staged rollout allows for gradual adoption and adjustment.

Launching and Scaling the DAO

Once the testing phase is successful, launch the ICP DAO. Develop a launch strategy that includes community announcements, incentivized participation, and educational resources. Monitor the initial stages of the DAO closely, addressing any challenges that arise. As the DAO gains momentum, explore opportunities for scalability, potentially through the introduction of subDAOs or the integration with other decentralized protocols.

Establishing Governance and Decision-Making Processes

As the DAO matures, establish clear governance processes for decision-making and evolution. Define the mechanisms for proposing and voting on changes to the DAO's smart contracts, tokenomics, and governance model. Consider introducing mechanisms for community-driven initiatives and funding proposals. Transparent governance processes contribute to the sustainability and adaptability of the DAO.

Measuring Success and Iterating

Regularly assess the performance and impact of the ICP DAO against predefined metrics and objectives.

Consider factors such as community participation, proposal success rates, and the overall health of the ecosystem. Solicit feedback from the community and use data-driven insights to iterate on the DAO model continuously. Embrace a culture of adaptability and continuous improvement.

Ensuring Regulatory Compliance

Navigate the legal landscape to ensure that the ICP DAO complies with relevant regulations. Consult legal experts to address issues related to tokenomics, data privacy, and financial compliance. Engage with regulators proactively, seeking clarity and contributing to the development of regulatory frameworks that support decentralized governance. Establish transparent and compliant practices to mitigate legal risks.

Conclusion: Paving the Way for Decentralized Innovation

Designing and implementing an ICP DAO is a dynamic and iterative process that requires a strategic blend of technical expertise, community engagement, and adaptability. By following a step-by-step approach, organizations and communities can unlock the transformative potential of decentralized governance within the Internet Computer Protocol ecosystem. As we conclude this guide, the final chapter will recap the transformative potential of ICP DAOs and issue a call to action for embracing the future of decentralized governance.

Community Engagement and Stakeholder Participation Strategies

In the realm of Internet Computer Protocol (ICP) Decentralized Autonomous Organizations (DAOs), success hinges on vibrant and active community engagement. This section delves into practical strategies for cultivating a thriving community and ensuring meaningful participation from stakeholders. Effective community engagement not only fosters inclusivity but also forms the bedrock for the sustained growth and impact of ICP DAOs.

Understanding the Significance of Community Engagement

Community engagement is the lifeblood of any DAO, representing the collective energy, ideas, and contributions of its members. It transcends mere participation and becomes a dynamic interaction between the DAO and its stakeholders. By recognizing the significance of community engagement, DAOs lay the groundwork for building a loyal and empowered user base that is actively involved in governance, decision-making, and the overall development of the ecosystem.

Building a Strong Foundation: Onboarding Strategies

The first step in effective community engagement is a seamless onboarding process. Ensure that new members can easily understand the DAO's mission, governance model, and how to participate. Develop educational resources, user guides, and interactive tutorials to familiarize newcomers with the DAO's structure and functions. A well-designed onboarding experience sets the tone for positive community engagement from the outset.

Open Channels of Communication: Creating Community Spaces

Establishing dedicated community spaces is essential for fostering communication and collaboration. Leverage platforms such as forums, chat groups, and social media to create inclusive spaces where community members can share ideas, ask questions, and connect with each other. Maintain an open and transparent dialogue to build a sense of belonging and empower members to actively contribute to discussions around governance, proposals, and community initiatives.

Inclusive Decision-Making: Community-Driven Governance

Empower community members by integrating community-driven governance mechanisms. Allow stakeholders to propose ideas, vote on proposals, and actively participate in shaping the direction of the DAO. Implement transparent decision-making processes that consider diverse perspectives and prioritize inclusivity. By involving the community in governance, DAOs not only decentralize decision-making but also strengthen the sense of ownership among stakeholders.

Rewarding Contributions: Incentive Mechanisms

Recognize and reward active contributions to incentivize ongoing participation. Implement incentive mechanisms such as token rewards, governance token distributions, or non-monetary rewards for community members who contribute meaningfully to the DAO. Creating a reward system not only acknowledges individual efforts but also encourages a culture of continuous engagement and collaboration.

Education and Awareness: Empowering the Community

Educating the community about the DAO's mission, governance processes, and broader ecosystem is crucial for informed participation. Develop educational initiatives, webinars, and documentation to empower community members with the knowledge needed to engage meaningfully. By fostering a culture of learning and awareness, DAOs create a community that is not only engaged but also equipped to actively contribute to the DAO's goals.

Community Feedback Loops: Gathering Input and Insights

Establishing effective feedback loops is instrumental in maintaining a responsive and adaptive community. Regularly solicit feedback from community members through surveys, polls, or dedicated feedback sessions. Actively listen to community input and use the insights gained to iterate on governance models, propose enhancements, or address concerns. This iterative approach ensures that the DAO evolves in alignment with the needs and aspirations of its community.

Collaborative Initiatives: Empowering Community-Driven Projects

Encourage and support community-driven projects and initiatives. Provide avenues for community members to propose and lead projects that align with the DAO's goals. Whether it's development, marketing, or community outreach, empowering individuals to take the lead fosters a sense of ownership and diversity within the community. Collaborative initiatives not only contribute to the DAO's objectives but also enrich the overall ecosystem.

Moderation and Community Management: Nurturing a Positive Environment

Effective community management is key to maintaining a positive and inclusive environment. Implement moderation strategies to ensure respectful discourse, prevent spam, and address any issues that may arise. Proactive community management sets the tone for a welcoming atmosphere, encouraging diverse perspectives and fostering a sense of unity among community members.

Events and Community Gatherings: Strengthening Connections

Organize events, virtual meetups, and conferences to facilitate real-time connections among community members. These gatherings provide opportunities for networking, knowledge sharing, and a deeper sense of community bonding. Hosting both online and offline events fosters a strong sense of belonging and camaraderie within the DAO, strengthening the social fabric of the community.

Measuring Community Metrics: Analytics for Growth

Utilize analytics and metrics to gauge the health and growth of the community. Track key indicators such as user engagement, participation rates, and sentiment analysis. Analyzing these metrics provides valuable insights into the effectiveness of community engagement strategies and helps identify areas for improvement. Data-driven decision-making ensures that community-building efforts align with the evolving needs of the DAO.

Global Outreach: Building a Diverse and Inclusive Community

Strive for global outreach to build a diverse and inclusive community. Engage with stakeholders from different geographic locations, cultures, and backgrounds. Implement strategies to overcome language barriers and ensure that information is accessible to a global audience. A diverse community not only enriches the pool of ideas but also strengthens the resilience and adaptability of the DAO.

Community Governance Support: Providing Resources and Guidance

Support community members who take on governance roles by providing resources, documentation, and mentorship. Empower governance participants with the tools and knowledge needed to effectively contribute to decision-making processes. Clear guidance enhances the effectiveness of community-driven governance and ensures that community members feel confident in their roles.

Celebrating Milestones: Acknowledging Community Achievements

Acknowledge and celebrate community milestones, whether they are related to governance decisions, collaborative projects, or individual achievements. Recognition fosters a positive and celebratory culture within the community, motivating members to continue their contributions. By publicly acknowledging achievements, DAOs reinforce the sense of community and inspire others to actively engage.

Adaptability and Continuous Improvement: Iterating for Success

Community engagement strategies should be dynamic and adaptable. Regularly assess the effectiveness of engagement initiatives and be open to iterating based on feedback and evolving community needs. Embrace a culture of continuous improvement, where lessons learned from previous engagements inform future strategies. The ability to adapt ensures that community engagement remains vibrant and responsive to the evolving dynamics of the DAO.

Conclusion: Nurturing a Thriving Community Ecosystem

In the tapestry of ICP DAOs, community engagement is the thread that weaves together diverse perspectives, ideas, and contributions. By implementing thoughtful strategies that prioritize inclusivity, empowerment, and collaboration, DAOs can cultivate a thriving community ecosystem. As we conclude this guide, the final chapter will recap the transformative potential of ICP DAOs and issue a call to action for embracing the future of decentralized governance.

Managing Risk and Mitigating Challenges in ICP DAOs

Implementing an Internet Computer Protocol (ICP) Decentralized Autonomous Organization (DAO) is a transformative journey, but it comes with its share of challenges and risks. This section explores proactive strategies for identifying, managing, and mitigating risks to ensure the robustness, security, and longevity of ICP DAOs.

Understanding the Landscape of Risks in DAOs

ICP DAOs operate in a dynamic and evolving ecosystem, facing a spectrum of risks that can impact their functionality, reputation, and community trust. Recognizing and categorizing these risks is the first step in implementing effective risk management strategies. The key categories of risks in ICP DAOs include technical, governance, security, legal and regulatory, and community-related risks.

Technical Risks: Building a Solid Foundation

Smart Contract Vulnerabilities: Smart contracts are the backbone of ICP DAOs, and vulnerabilities in their code can lead to exploits and security breaches. Mitigate this risk by conducting thorough code audits, implementing best practices in smart contract development, and staying informed about emerging security standards. Engage with the community and external auditors to ensure a diverse set of eyes on the codebase.

Compatibility and Integration Risks: ICP DAOs may rely on various technologies and platforms, and changes in the broader ecosystem can introduce compatibility issues. Regularly assess compatibility risks and stay informed about updates or changes in the ICP ecosystem. Implement robust testing protocols to ensure seamless integration with evolving technologies and platforms.

Scalability Challenges: As ICP DAOs grow, scalability challenges may emerge, affecting transaction throughput and response times. Design DAO architecture with scalability in mind, leveraging features such as subnets and optimizing smart contract execution. Monitor network performance and be prepared to implement scaling solutions as the DAO expands.

Governance Risks: Navigating Decision-Making Complexity

Governance Model Risks: The governance model chosen for the DAO can introduce risks related to centralization, inefficiency, or lack of inclusivity. Regularly evaluate the effectiveness of the chosen governance model and be open to adjustments based on community feedback.

Strive for a balance that ensures decentralized decision-making while maintaining efficiency.

Voter Apathy and Inactivity: Low voter turnout or apathy can hinder the effectiveness of governance processes. Implement strategies to incentivize voter participation, such as governance token rewards, and foster a culture of community engagement. Educate the community about the impact of their participation on the DAO's direction and outcomes.

Decision Deadlocks: In complex decision-making structures, deadlocks can occur when there is an impasse in reaching consensus. Establish clear protocols for resolving deadlocks, including mechanisms for tie-breaking votes or dispute resolution. Encourage community discussions to address contentious issues before they escalate into deadlocks.

Security Risks: Safeguarding Assets and Data

Smart Contract Exploits: Security vulnerabilities in smart contracts can lead to exploits, potentially resulting in the loss of assets. Conduct regular security audits, implement best practices in smart contract development, and encourage the community to report potential vulnerabilities through bug bounty programs. Develop emergency response plans in case of security incidents.

Malicious Attacks: ICP DAOs may become targets for malicious attacks, including Distributed Denial of Service (DDoS) attacks or hacking attempts. Implement robust security measures, including firewalls, encryption, and multi-factor authentication, to protect the DAO's infrastructure. Collaborate with security experts and leverage threat intelligence to stay ahead of potential threats.

Asset Custody Risks: The custody of assets within the DAO, such as governance tokens or funds, poses inherent risks. Implement secure multi-signature wallets, consider third-party custody solutions, and regularly assess and update security protocols. Transparently communicate security measures to the community to build trust in the DAO's asset management practices.

Legal and Regulatory Risks: Navigating Compliance Challenges

Uncertain Regulatory Landscape: The decentralized nature of DAOs introduces complexities in navigating the legal and regulatory landscape. Stay informed about developments in blockchain and cryptocurrency regulations globally. Engage with legal experts to assess the DAO's compliance with relevant laws and proactively seek legal opinions on key matters.

Intellectual Property Concerns: As DAOs evolve, issues related to intellectual property (IP) may arise, particularly in projects involving creative content or unique innovations. Clarify ownership and licensing arrangements within the DAO's governance framework. Consider legal mechanisms, such as smart contracts or decentralized autonomous copyright organizations, to address IP concerns.

Tax Implications: Tax regulations for cryptocurrency transactions and governance token holdings can vary across jurisdictions. Collaborate with tax experts to understand the tax implications of DAO activities for both the DAO and its community members. Implement transparent reporting mechanisms and educate the community about their potential tax obligations.

Community-Related Risks: Fostering Inclusivity and Trust

Community Discord and Disagreements: Community disagreements and discord can impact the cohesion of the DAO. Foster a culture of open communication and respect diverse opinions. Implement community moderation strategies to address conflicts in a constructive manner. Establish clear community guidelines and codes of conduct to maintain a positive and inclusive atmosphere.

Token Distribution Imbalances: Unequal distribution of governance tokens can lead to concentration of power and influence within the DAO. Strive for a fair and decentralized token distribution model from the outset. Consider mechanisms such as token vesting and progressive decentralization to prevent concentration and encourage wider participation.

Community Trust Erosion: Events such as security incidents, governance controversies, or perceived unfairness can erode community trust. Prioritize transparency in communication, actively address community concerns, and implement mechanisms for community feedback. Trust is foundational to the success of a DAO, and maintaining open channels of communication is key to preserving it.

Proactive Risk Management Strategies

Continuous Risk Assessment: Regularly assess and reassess the landscape of risks facing the DAO. Stay informed about emerging threats, regulatory developments, and changes in the broader blockchain ecosystem. Implement a continuous risk assessment process to identify and evaluate new risks as they arise.

Emergency Response Plans: Develop comprehensive emergency response plans outlining steps to be taken in the event of security incidents, governance crises, or other emergencies. Establish communication protocols to keep the community informed and engaged during emergency situations. Conduct periodic drills to ensure readiness.

Insurance and Risk Mitigation Instruments: Explore the availability of insurance products and risk mitigation instruments tailored for DAOs. While the decentralized nature of DAOs presents challenges for traditional insurance, new solutions are emerging to cover risks such as smart contract exploits and asset losses. Collaborate with insurance providers to assess and implement suitable coverage.

Community Education and Empowerment: Educate the community about potential risks and empower them with the knowledge needed to make informed decisions. Implement educational initiatives, webinars, and documentation to raise awareness about security best practices, governance processes, and legal considerations. Informed community members are better equipped to contribute to risk mitigation.

Legal Compliance Audits: Engage legal experts to conduct regular compliance audits, ensuring that the DAO remains in adherence to relevant laws and regulations. Include legal compliance as part of routine governance activities, and be proactive in seeking legal opinions on key decisions or initiatives that may have legal implications.

Conclusion: Navigating the Path to Long-Term Success

Navigating the risks inherent in implementing ICP DAOs requires a proactive and holistic approach. By understanding the diverse landscape of risks and implementing strategic risk management measures, DAOs can safeguard their functionality, protect assets, and build resilience in the face of challenges. As we conclude this guide, the final chapter will recap the transformative potential of ICP DAOs and issue a call to action for embracing the future of decentralized governance.

Measuring Success and Assessing Impact: Evaluating the Performance of ICP DAOs

The journey of implementing an Internet Computer Protocol (ICP) Decentralized Autonomous Organization (DAO) is not only about establishing structures and processes but also about continuously measuring success and assessing impact. In this section, we explore the key metrics, methodologies, and considerations involved in evaluating the performance of ICP DAOs.

Understanding Success in the Context of DAOs

Before delving into specific metrics, it's essential to define what success means for an ICP DAO. Success in this context extends beyond traditional business metrics and encompasses the fulfillment of the DAO's mission, effective governance, community engagement, and the achievement of predefined objectives. Success is multifaceted, involving both quantitative and qualitative aspects that contribute to the DAO's overall impact on the decentralized ecosystem.

Key Performance Indicators (KPIs) for ICP DAOs

KPI 1: Governance Participation Rate

- Definition: The percentage of eligible community members actively participating in governance processes, including proposal voting and decision-making.

- Significance: Reflects the level of community engagement and the effectiveness of the DAO's governance model.

- Measurement: Calculated as (Number of Participants / Total Eligible Members) * 100.

KPI 2: Proposal Approval Rate

- Definition: The percentage of proposed changes or initiatives that are approved through community voting.

- Significance: Indicates the efficiency and responsiveness of the governance process in implementing community-driven decisions.

- Measurement: Calculated as (Number of Approved Proposals / Total Number of Proposals) * 100.

KPI 3: Community Growth Rate

- Definition: The rate at which the DAO's community is expanding, including new members joining community spaces and participating in governance.

- Significance: Reflects the DAO's ability to attract and retain a diverse and engaged community.

- Measurement: Calculated as ((Current Community Size - Previous Community Size) / Previous Community Size) * 100.

KPI 4: Token Distribution Equality

- Definition: The measure of how evenly governance tokens are distributed among community members.

- Significance: Addresses the risk of token concentration and promotes a more decentralized governance structure.

- Measurement: Utilize metrics such as Gini coefficient or concentration ratios to assess token distribution equality.

KPI 5: Smart Contract Security Rating

- Definition: An assessment of the security robustness of the DAO's smart contracts, considering factors such as code audits, vulnerabilities, and historical exploits.

- Significance: Provides insights into the security posture of the DAO's technical foundation.

- Measurement: Collaborate with security experts to conduct periodic smart contract audits and assessments.

KPI 6: Community Sentiment Analysis

- Definition: The analysis of community sentiment through social media, forums, and other communication channels.

- Significance: Gauges the overall mood and perception of the community, offering qualitative insights into their satisfaction and concerns.

- Measurement: Utilize sentiment analysis tools or community surveys to assess sentiment trends.

KPI 7: Governance Decision Turnaround Time

- Definition: The average time taken to make decisions through the governance process, from proposal submission to implementation.
- Significance: Reflects the efficiency of the governance process and its ability to respond to community needs in a timely manner.
- Measurement: Calculate the average time for recent governance decisions.

KPI 8: Contribution Recognition Index

- Definition: A metric reflecting the extent to which community contributions are recognized and rewarded, considering factors such as governance proposals, projects, and collaborations.
- Significance: Encourages and acknowledges community participation, fostering a culture of contribution.
- Measurement: Develop a scoring system or use community feedback to assess the impact and recognition of individual contributions.

Methodologies for Impact Assessment

Qualitative Impact Assessments: Conduct qualitative assessments to understand the broader impact of the DAO on its community and the decentralized ecosystem. Gather narratives, testimonials, and case studies to highlight success stories, community initiatives, and positive outcomes resulting from the DAO's activities.

Community Surveys and Feedback: Regularly solicit feedback from community members through surveys and feedback sessions. Gather insights into community satisfaction, identify areas for improvement, and assess the perceived impact of the DAO on individual stakeholders.

Community Case Studies: Develop and showcase case studies highlighting specific community-driven projects, governance decisions, or initiatives that have had a tangible impact. Illustrate how the DAO's actions translate into real-world outcomes and positive changes.

External Validation and Recognition: Seek external validation through partnerships, collaborations, or recognition from industry experts and stakeholders. External endorsements can serve as indicators of the DAO's influence and positive impact on the wider decentralized landscape.

Challenges in Assessing DAO Impact

Subjectivity in Success Metrics: Defining success metrics for DAOs involves a degree of subjectivity, as different stakeholders may prioritize different aspects of success. Strive for a balanced approach that considers both quantitative metrics and qualitative assessments.

Long-Term Impact Measurement: Assessing the long-term impact of DAOs is challenging, as some outcomes may take time to materialize. Develop mechanisms for tracking and evaluating impact over extended periods, considering the evolving nature of the decentralized space.

Community Diversity Considerations: Metrics such as community growth and engagement should consider the diversity of the community. Ensure that growth initiatives are inclusive and that engagement metrics reflect contributions from a broad spectrum of community members.

Evolving Ecosystem Dynamics: The decentralized ecosystem is dynamic and subject to rapid changes. Adapt impact assessment strategies to account for evolving technologies, market trends, and regulatory developments that may influence the DAO's performance.

Conclusion: Navigating the Journey of Impactful Governance

Measuring the success and impact of ICP DAOs requires a thoughtful blend of quantitative metrics and qualitative assessments. By regularly evaluating key performance indicators, leveraging impact assessment methodologies, and addressing inherent challenges, DAOs can refine their strategies, adapt to evolving community needs, and continue to be impactful players in the decentralized governance landscape. As we conclude this guide, the final chapter will recap the transformative potential of ICP DAOs and issue a call to action for embracing the future of decentralized governance.

Conclusion

Recapping the Transformative Potential of ICP DAOs – A Paradigm Shift in Governance

In the preceding chapters, we embarked on a comprehensive exploration of the Internet Computer Protocol (ICP) Decentralized Autonomous Organizations (DAOs), delving into their technological foundations, mechanics, real-world applications, future possibilities, legal considerations, practical implementation, and risk management. As we bring this journey to a close, it is imperative to recap the transformative potential of ICP DAOs and understand their role in reshaping the landscape of governance.

The Evolution of Governance: Unveiling the Power of DAOs

The advent of blockchain technology ushered in a new era of decentralized governance, challenging traditional hierarchical structures and placing decision-making power back into the hands of communities. ICP DAOs stand at the forefront of this evolution, leveraging innovative technologies and governance models to redefine how organizations operate, make decisions, and interact with their stakeholders.

At the heart of this paradigm shift is the concept of DAOs as autonomous, community-driven entities. Unlike centralized structures where power is concentrated in a few hands, ICP DAOs distribute governance authority among their community members, fostering inclusivity, transparency, and collective decision-making. This shift challenges long-standing norms, offering a glimpse into a future where individuals actively participate in shaping the organizations they engage with.

The Essence of ICP DAOs: A Technological Marvel

The technological foundation of ICP DAOs is built on pillars that ensure resilience, security, and scalability. Canister smart contracts serve as the building blocks, executing code in a decentralized and tamper-resistant manner. Chain-key cryptography secures the very foundations of the DAO system, providing a robust framework for trust and integrity. Asynchronous Byzantine Fault Tolerance (aBFT) ensures network resilience, safeguarding against malicious actors and ensuring the continuous operation of the DAO. Subnets contribute to the diversity and scalability of the ICP DAO ecosystem, enabling a dynamic and adaptable infrastructure.

These technological marvels are not merely technical intricacies; they represent the tools that empower communities to govern themselves. Canisters enable the execution of community-approved code without intermediaries, ensuring that the DAO operates according to the will of its stakeholders. Chain-key cryptography guarantees the integrity of the DAO's operations, building trust among community members. aBFT, through its consensus mechanism, lays the foundation for a secure and resilient governance system. Subnets provide the flexibility needed to accommodate diverse use cases and adapt to the ever-changing landscape of decentralized governance.

The Pulse of ICP Governance: Network Nervous System (NNS)

Central to the ICP DAO ecosystem is the Network Nervous System (NNS), serving as the pulse that orchestrates the various components of governance. NNS is not merely a technical component; it is the embodiment of community-driven decision-making. Through the NNS, community members propose and vote on changes to the network, influencing its direction and evolution. The NNS represents a direct channel through which the collective intelligence of the community manifests in the governance of the ICP ecosystem.

As we navigate the intricacies of the NNS, we find a governance model that transcends traditional boundaries. It is a model that values participation, decentralization, and adaptability. Through the NNS, decisions are made collectively, aligning the interests of the community with the trajectory of the DAO. This model goes beyond the conventional notions of governance, transforming it into a dynamic and responsive process shaped by the diverse perspectives of its participants.

Mechanics of ICP DAOs: Empowering Community Participation

The mechanics of ICP DAOs are designed with a singular focus: empowering community participation. The proposal creation and voting process form the core of this empowerment, allowing community members to actively contribute to decision-making. This democratic approach ensures that the governance of ICP DAOs is a reflection of the collective will of the community.

Governance tokenomics further align incentives, turning community members into stakeholders with a vested interest in the success of the DAO. As DAOs evolve and adapt to the dynamic landscape, the mechanics ensure that the governance structures remain responsive and resilient. The security of ICP DAOs is not just a technical consideration but a holistic approach that protects assets and maintains the trust bestowed upon the DAO by its community.

ICP DAOs in Action: Impacting Real-World Applications

Beyond the technical intricacies, ICP DAOs are making tangible impacts in diverse real-world applications. In the realm of non-profit organizations, community-driven governance is redefining how social impact initiatives are conceived and executed. The intersection of decentralized finance (DeFi) and ICP DAOs is reshaping the financial services landscape, unlocking new possibilities for inclusion and accessibility. ICP DAOs are proving to be catalysts for positive social impact and community initiatives, harnessing the power of decentralized governance for the greater good. In the arts and entertainment sector, creativity and innovation are flourishing under the influence of ICP DAOs, showcasing the potential for decentralized governance to permeate every facet of human endeavor.

These real-world applications exemplify the versatility and adaptability of ICP DAOs. They are not confined to a single industry or use case but are rather a canvas upon which communities paint their visions for a more equitable and collaborative future.

The Future of ICP DAOs: A Vision for Decentralized Governance

Looking ahead, the future of ICP DAOs is characterized by an evolving governance paradigm. These DAOs are not static entities; they are living organisms that respond to the needs and aspirations of their communities. Evolving governance models redefine the boundaries of what is possible, showcasing ICP DAOs as a paradigm for modern governance.

Addressing the challenges of scalability and sustainability becomes crucial for the continued growth and relevance of ICP DAOs. As the user base expands and new use cases emerge, scalability ensures that the DAOs can handle increased demands without compromising performance. Sustainability goes beyond technical considerations, encompassing economic, environmental, and social dimensions. ICP DAOs are not just tools for governance; they are instruments for inclusivity, empowerment, and positive impact.

Interoperability and ecosystem integration amplify the influence of ICP DAOs by connecting them to the wider blockchain landscape. In a world where collaboration and connectivity are paramount, the ability of DAOs to seamlessly interact with other blockchain networks fosters a more interconnected and interoperable decentralized ecosystem.

Empowering individuals and communities is the ultimate goal of ICP DAOs. These entities are not just reshaping governance; they are rewriting the narrative of collective agency. Inclusive governance becomes a powerful tool for addressing societal challenges, fostering innovation, and building resilient communities.

Legal and Regulatory Considerations: Navigating Complexity

Amidst the transformative potential of ICP DAOs, the legal and regulatory landscape introduces a layer of complexity. Navigating this landscape requires a nuanced understanding of the regulatory framework for ICP DAOs. Intellectual property rights (IPR) become a focal point in protecting innovation in the digital age, while considerations of taxation and financial compliance add layers of responsibility to DAO operations.

Data privacy and security, paramount in the digital era, demand careful attention to protect user data within the ICP DAO ecosystem. As DAOs navigate this complex terrain, they contribute to the ongoing dialogue on how decentralized governance can coexist with and adapt to existing legal frameworks.

Realizing the Potential of ICP DAOs: A Practical Guide

Implementing ICP DAOs is not just a theoretical endeavor; it is a practical guide for transforming ideals into reality. Designing and implementing an ICP DAO involves a step-by-step approach that considers technical, social, and economic factors. Community engagement and stakeholder participation strategies become essential elements in ensuring that the DAO reflects the diverse voices and perspectives of its members.

Yet, as with any transformative journey, risks and challenges abound. Managing risk and mitigating challenges in ICP DAOs require a proactive and holistic approach. By understanding the diverse landscape of risks and implementing strategic risk management measures, DAOs can safeguard their functionality, protect assets, and build resilience in the face of challenges.

Measuring Success and Assessing Impact: A Continuous Journey

Success in the realm of ICP DAOs is not a destination; it is a continuous journey. Measuring success and assessing impact involve a dynamic interplay of quantitative metrics and qualitative assessments. Key performance indicators (KPIs) serve as navigational tools, offering insights into governance participation, proposal approval rates, community growth, and the distribution of governance tokens.

Beyond metrics, methodologies for impact assessment add depth to the understanding of a DAO's influence. Qualitative assessments, community surveys, case studies, and external validation contribute to a comprehensive evaluation of the DAO's performance and impact.

Conclusion: A Call to Action for Embracing the Future

As we recapture the transformative potential of ICP DAOs, it becomes evident that we are standing at the cusp of a paradigm shift in governance. The journey has unveiled a decentralized future where communities actively shape the organizations they engage with. ICP DAOs, with their innovative technologies, robust mechanics, and real-world impact, are pioneers in this transformative journey.

Addressing future challenges and opportunities is not a distant task but a call to action for all stakeholders in the decentralized ecosystem. Whether developers, community members, regulators, or innovators, each has a role in shaping the trajectory of ICP DAOs. Embracing this future requires a collective commitment to inclusivity, resilience, and the continual pursuit of positive impact.

In this decentralized future, ICP DAOs stand as beacons of possibility, guiding the way for others to follow.

As we conclude this exploration, let us embark on the journey ahead with a shared vision of decentralized governance that empowers individuals, fosters collaboration, and builds a more equitable and sustainable future. The transformative potential of ICP DAOs is not just a theoretical concept; it is a call to action for everyone invested in the future of governance.

Addressing Future Challenges and Opportunities - Paving the Way for Widespread Adoption

As we stand at the culmination of this exploration into the transformative potential of Internet Computer Protocol (ICP) Decentralized Autonomous Organizations (DAOs), it is essential to cast our gaze forward and discern the path that lies ahead. The decentralized governance landscape is dynamic, constantly evolving, presenting both challenges and opportunities that will shape the future of ICP DAOs and, by extension, the broader decentralized ecosystem. In this concluding chapter, we address the future with a focus on overcoming challenges and embracing opportunities to pave the way for widespread adoption.

Embracing the Evolution of Governance Models

The evolution of governance models is at the forefront of the future trajectory of ICP DAOs. Traditional governance structures are being challenged, and DAOs are positioned as trailblazers in redefining how decisions are made and power is distributed. As the decentralized space matures, governance models will continue to evolve, necessitating a nimble and adaptive approach. ICP DAOs, with their emphasis on community-driven decision-making, are well-positioned to influence and contribute to the ongoing discourse on effective governance models in the digital age.

An essential aspect of this evolution involves experimenting with new governance mechanisms. ICP DAOs can serve as laboratories for testing innovative ideas, such as quadratic voting, prediction markets, and other mechanisms that enhance community participation and decision-making accuracy. By embracing experimentation, DAOs contribute not only to their own growth but also to the collective understanding of what works best in decentralized governance.

Scalability and Sustainability: Imperatives for Growth

As the user base and the scope of ICP DAOs expand, scalability becomes a critical factor. The ability of these DAOs to handle increased transactions, participants, and complexity without sacrificing performance is paramount. Scalability goes beyond technological considerations and extends to economic, social, and environmental dimensions.

Ensuring economic scalability involves designing incentive structures that accommodate a growing and diverse user base. As more individuals and communities engage with ICP DAOs, the economic mechanisms must remain inclusive and adaptive. This inclusivity is not only about providing access but also about creating economic models that benefit a wide spectrum of participants, fostering a sense of ownership and shared success.

Social scalability, on the other hand, entails developing governance structures that can effectively accommodate a larger and more diverse community. As the number of stakeholders increases, DAOs must evolve to maintain a balance between inclusivity and efficiency. Mechanisms for meaningful participation, transparent decision-making, and effective communication become central to achieving social scalability.

Environmental sustainability is a consideration that aligns with the broader discourse on responsible and eco-friendly blockchain technologies. ICP DAOs, like other blockchain networks, should explore and adopt energy-efficient consensus mechanisms and eco-conscious practices. By prioritizing sustainability, DAOs contribute to the broader narrative of responsible technology and align with the growing societal emphasis on environmental consciousness.

Interoperability and Ecosystem Integration: Building Bridges Across Blockchains

The future of ICP DAOs is intricately linked with their ability to interact seamlessly with other blockchain networks. Interoperability emerges as a key theme, emphasizing the importance of building bridges that connect ICP DAOs to the wider decentralized ecosystem. In a landscape characterized by a multitude of blockchains, each with its unique strengths and use cases, interoperability becomes a catalyst for collaboration and innovation.

Interoperability enables assets, data, and functionalities to move seamlessly between different blockchains. ICP DAOs, by fostering interoperability, position themselves as integral components of a larger decentralized network. This interconnectedness amplifies the impact of DAOs, allowing them to leverage the strengths of other blockchains, access a broader user base, and contribute to a more cohesive and collaborative decentralized ecosystem.

Ecosystem integration extends beyond technical interoperability and involves active collaboration with projects and communities on other blockchains. Establishing partnerships, participating in cross-chain initiatives, and aligning with shared objectives contribute to a more vibrant and interconnected decentralized landscape. ICP DAOs, as pioneers in decentralized governance, have the opportunity to play a leading role in shaping cross-chain collaborations and contributing to the development of interoperable standards.

Empowering Individuals and Communities: A Continual Imperative

At the core of ICP DAOs lies the mission of empowering individuals and communities. This imperative extends beyond the immediate community of DAO participants to encompass a broader societal impact. As DAOs continue to evolve, strategies for empowerment should be dynamic, adaptive, and inclusive.

Inclusivity in DAOs involves actively seeking diversity in participation, ensuring that governance structures accommodate voices from various backgrounds, cultures, and perspectives. Strategies for inclusivity go beyond accessibility and involve intentional efforts to address barriers that may prevent certain groups from engaging with DAOs. By fostering a diverse and inclusive community, DAOs contribute to the creation of more robust and resilient governance systems.

Education emerges as a key component of empowerment. Providing resources, documentation, and educational initiatives helps community members understand the intricacies of governance, smart contracts, and the broader blockchain ecosystem. Empowered individuals are not just passive participants but active contributors who shape the trajectory of DAOs and drive meaningful impact.

Financial inclusivity remains a cornerstone of empowerment. ICP DAOs should explore mechanisms that democratize access to governance tokens, allowing a broader audience to participate in decision-making processes. As DAOs become more ingrained in societal structures, the ability to empower individuals economically becomes a transformative force for positive change.

Legal and Regulatory Considerations: Navigating a Dynamic Landscape

The future of ICP DAOs is inevitably entwined with the evolving legal and regulatory landscape. As decentralized governance gains prominence, regulators are grappling with how to navigate this novel paradigm. ICP DAOs, along with other decentralized entities, have the opportunity to engage proactively with regulatory bodies, contributing to the development of frameworks that strike a balance between innovation and compliance.

A collaborative approach involves fostering dialogue between DAOs, legal experts, and regulatory authorities. Establishing clear communication channels, participating in regulatory consultations, and providing insights into the functioning of DAOs can contribute to the creation of informed and constructive regulations. This proactive engagement positions DAOs as responsible actors in the broader regulatory discourse.

Intellectual Property Rights (IPR) in the digital age become a critical consideration for DAOs that are often at the forefront of technological innovation. Establishing frameworks for protecting and acknowledging intellectual property within DAOs ensures that creators and contributors are incentivized and rewarded for their innovations. ICP DAOs, by actively addressing IPR concerns, contribute to a legal environment that fosters creativity and innovation.

Navigating taxation and financial compliance is an ongoing challenge for DAOs. As regulatory bodies develop tax frameworks for decentralized entities, DAOs must stay informed, engage with tax professionals, and proactively adhere to compliance requirements. Transparency in financial operations and collaboration with regulatory bodies contribute to a regulatory landscape that is conducive to the continued growth of ICP DAOs.

Data privacy and security considerations are paramount in the digital era. DAOs should adopt robust measures to protect user data, ensuring compliance with data protection regulations. By prioritizing data privacy and security, DAOs build trust among community members and contribute to the broader narrative of responsible and ethical technology.

Realizing the Potential: A Practical Guide for Implementation

Realizing the potential of ICP DAOs requires a practical guide for implementation. Designing and implementing an ICP DAO involves a step-by-step approach that encompasses technical, social, and economic dimensions. This practical guide serves as a roadmap for developers, community members, and stakeholders involved in the creation and sustenance of ICP DAOs.

The process begins with defining the purpose and scope of the DAO. Clearly articulating the objectives, use cases, and community values provides a foundational understanding for all stakeholders. Designing the DAO's governance structure follows, involving decisions on voting mechanisms, tokenomics, and decision-making processes. Community engagement strategies are integral to ensuring that the governance model reflects the diverse perspectives of stakeholders.

Implementation involves the deployment of smart contracts and the establishment of the DAO's technical infrastructure. The choice of consensus mechanisms, security protocols, and interoperability considerations becomes crucial at this stage. Rigorous testing and auditing contribute to the creation of a secure and resilient DAO.

Community engagement and stakeholder participation strategies play a continual role in the implementation phase. Ongoing communication, education initiatives, and mechanisms for gathering feedback ensure that the DAO remains responsive to the needs of its community. The empowerment of community members involves not just participation in decision-making but also opportunities for governance token ownership and economic involvement.

Risk management is an integral part of the implementation guide. Identifying potential risks, whether technical, economic, or social, allows DAOs to proactively address challenges and build resilience. The practical guide should include methodologies for risk assessment, contingency planning, and continuous monitoring to ensure the sustained functionality of the DAO.

Measuring success and assessing impact form the final stages of the implementation guide. Establishing key performance indicators (KPIs) that align with the DAO's objectives allows for quantitative evaluation of performance. Qualitative assessments, including community surveys, case studies, and external validation, provide a holistic understanding of the DAO's impact on its community and the broader ecosystem.

Conclusion: A Call to Action for Widespread Adoption

In conclusion, the future of ICP DAOs is a call to action for widespread adoption. As we navigate the challenges and opportunities that lie ahead, it is evident that the transformative potential of DAOs extends beyond a niche technology to a fundamental shift in how societies govern themselves. The call to action involves active participation from developers, community members, regulators, and innovators in embracing decentralized governance as a cornerstone of the digital age.

Widespread adoption is not a distant goal but a collective endeavor that requires collaboration, inclusivity, and a shared commitment to the principles of decentralization. Developers play a crucial role in refining the technological foundations of ICP DAOs, ensuring scalability, security, and interoperability. Community members contribute to the vibrancy of DAOs by actively engaging in governance, sharing insights, and fostering a culture of collaboration.

Regulators are invited to participate in the ongoing dialogue, recognizing the potential of decentralized governance while collaboratively shaping frameworks that balance innovation with legal compliance. Innovators are encouraged to explore new frontiers, experiment with governance models, and contribute to the continual evolution of decentralized ecosystems.

As we heed this call to action, the transformative potential of ICP DAOs becomes not just a theoretical concept but a lived reality, reshaping governance, fostering empowerment, and paving the way for a decentralized future. The journey ahead is one of continuous growth, adaptation, and collaboration, and by answering this call, we collectively contribute to the dawn of a new era in governance, guided by the principles of decentralization, transparency, and community empowerment.

A Call to Action: Embracing the Future of Decentralized Governance with ICP DAOs

In the closing chapters of this exploration into the transformative potential of Internet Computer Protocol (ICP) Decentralized Autonomous Organizations (DAOs), a resounding call to action emerges. As we reflect on the journey through the dawn of decentralized governance, the essence of the ICP DAO system, and the intricate mechanics that power it, the imperative becomes clear—this is not merely a technological evolution but a paradigm shift in governance. This call to action is an invitation to stakeholders across the spectrum, from developers and community members to regulators and innovators, to actively embrace the future of decentralized governance with ICP DAOs.

The Essence of ICP DAOs: Shaping a Paradigm for Modern Governance

At the heart of the call to action is the recognition of ICP DAOs as architects of a new governance paradigm. It goes beyond the mere deployment of cutting-edge technologies; it encompasses a fundamental redefinition of how decisions are made, power is distributed, and communities engage with the organizations that impact their lives. The essence of ICP DAOs lies in their ability to embody principles of decentralization, transparency, and community-driven decision-making, setting the stage for a more inclusive and equitable future.

As we heed this call, we acknowledge that the essence of ICP DAOs is not confined to the digital realm; it extends into the fabric of societal structures. ICP DAOs are catalysts for reimagining governance at its core, fostering a shift from centralized, top-down structures to decentralized, bottom-up models. This shift is an invitation for individuals and communities to actively participate in the decisions that affect them, transcending geographical boundaries and cultural differences.

Embracing a Dynamic Landscape: A Continuous Evolution

The call to action is a beckoning towards embracing the dynamic landscape of decentralized governance. ICP DAOs, as pioneers in this space, are not static entities but living organisms that evolve in response to the needs of their communities and the challenges of the broader ecosystem. This evolution necessitates a mindset of continual learning, adaptation, and innovation.

Developers, as the architects of the technological foundations of ICP DAOs, play a crucial role in embracing this dynamic landscape. The call is for ongoing refinement of smart contracts, exploration of novel consensus mechanisms, and a commitment to scalability, security, and interoperability. The ever-changing nature of the decentralized landscape demands a proactive approach to staying at the forefront of technological advancements.

Community members, as active participants in ICP DAOs, are called to embrace the evolving nature of governance structures. This involves not only engaging in decision-making processes but also contributing to the cultural and social aspects of DAOs. The call is for inclusive participation, diverse perspectives, and a commitment to building resilient and vibrant communities.

Regulators, too, are invited to navigate this dynamic landscape with an open and collaborative mindset. Recognizing the potential of decentralized governance, the call is for a regulatory framework that balances the need for innovation with considerations of legal compliance. Engaging in ongoing dialogue with DAOs and the broader decentralized ecosystem ensures that regulations evolve in tandem with the technology they govern.

The Imperative of Inclusive Governance: Empowering Individuals and Communities

A central tenet of the call to action is the imperative of inclusive governance. ICP DAOs stand as beacons of inclusivity, inviting individuals and communities to actively participate in shaping the organizations they engage with. This inclusivity extends beyond the realm of technology; it is a societal imperative that empowers diverse voices and perspectives.

Developers are called to design and implement governance structures that prioritize inclusivity. This involves not only providing access but actively seeking diversity in participation. The call is for mechanisms that address barriers to entry, whether they be technological, linguistic, or cultural, ensuring that a wide spectrum of individuals can engage meaningfully with ICP DAOs.

Community members are invited to embrace the responsibility of fostering inclusivity within DAOs. This goes beyond individual participation in governance; it involves creating a culture of respect, openness, and acceptance. The call is for active engagement in initiatives that promote diversity, equity, and inclusion, ensuring that the benefits of decentralized governance are accessible to all.

Regulators, too, play a role in promoting inclusive governance by recognizing the diverse nature of decentralized communities. The call is for regulatory frameworks that do not inadvertently exclude certain groups or hinder the participatory nature of DAOs. Engaging with

DAOs to understand their unique challenges and opportunities is crucial in fostering a regulatory environment that aligns with the principles of inclusivity.

Scaling Heights: Addressing Challenges and Fostering Growth

The call to action entails a collective commitment to scaling new heights while acknowledging and addressing the challenges that lie in the ascent. ICP DAOs, as they grow in prominence, face challenges that span technological, economic, social, and regulatory dimensions. The call is for a resilient and adaptive approach to overcoming these challenges, fostering sustainable growth and widespread adoption.

Technologically, the call is for developers to continue pushing the boundaries of innovation. Scalability, security, and interoperability are not static goals but evolving benchmarks that require continual refinement. The challenge is to navigate the complexities of decentralized technologies while maintaining a focus on user experience and accessibility.

Economically, the call is for the creation of models that ensure the sustainability of DAOs. This involves designing incentive structures that align with the long-term success of the organization. The challenge is to balance economic scalability with principles of fairness, ensuring that economic participation is inclusive and beneficial to a broad spectrum of stakeholders.

Socially, the call is for the evolution of governance models that accommodate a growing and diverse community. As DAOs expand, the challenge is to maintain a sense of community and meaningful participation. Mechanisms for effective communication, transparent decision-making, and dispute resolution become paramount in addressing the social challenges of growth.

Regulatorily, the call is for collaborative efforts to navigate the evolving legal landscape. DAOs and regulators are partners in shaping a regulatory framework that facilitates innovation while safeguarding against potential risks. The challenge is to establish a dialogue that fosters understanding and collaboration, ensuring that regulations evolve in tandem with the dynamic nature of decentralized governance.

Interconnected Horizons: Building Bridges in the Decentralized Ecosystem

The call to action resonates with the imperative of building bridges in the decentralized ecosystem. ICP DAOs are not isolated entities; they exist within a broader landscape of blockchain networks, decentralized applications, and diverse communities. The call is for interconnected horizons, where DAOs actively collaborate, learn from each other, and contribute to the collective growth of the decentralized space.

Technologically, the call is for interoperability—the ability of ICP DAOs to seamlessly interact with other blockchain networks. This involves building bridges that facilitate the flow of assets, data, and functionalities across different decentralized ecosystems. The challenge is to create standards and protocols that enable interoperability, fostering a more connected and collaborative decentralized landscape.

Economically, the call is for ecosystem integration— the active collaboration of ICP DAOs with projects and communities on other blockchains. This involves partnerships, joint initiatives, and a commitment to shared objectives. The challenge is to break down silos, overcome tribalism, and recognize the interconnectedness of decentralized entities in creating a more vibrant and cohesive ecosystem.

Socially, the call is for community-building that transcends individual DAOs. Interconnected horizons involve shared values, collective initiatives, and a sense of solidarity among decentralized communities. The challenge is to foster a spirit of collaboration, where lessons learned in one DAO benefit others, and a collective ethos of support and cooperation prevails.

Regulatorily, the call is for collaborative frameworks that facilitate cross-chain interactions. As ICP DAOs engage with regulators, the challenge is to advocate for regulations that consider the cross-cutting nature of decentralized technologies. Building bridges with regulatory bodies ensures that regulations are not isolated but contribute to the creation of a harmonized and interoperable decentralized landscape.

Embodying Principles: Responsible Innovation and Ethical Governance

The call to action is a summons to embody principles of responsible innovation and ethical governance. ICP DAOs, as trailblazers in decentralized governance, are positioned to set standards for the responsible use of technology and the ethical conduct of decentralized organizations. This entails a commitment to values that prioritize the well-being of individuals, communities, and the broader ecosystem.

Technologically, responsible innovation involves considering the broader societal impact of technological advancements. The call is for developers to actively assess the potential risks and benefits of new features, consensus mechanisms, and smart contract functionalities. The challenge is to adopt a precautionary approach, ensuring that technological innovations align with principles of transparency, security, and user privacy.

Economically, responsible innovation extends to the design of tokenomics and economic models. This involves a commitment to fairness, avoiding exploitative practices, and creating economic structures that benefit a wide spectrum of participants. The challenge is to prioritize economic inclusivity, ensuring that the benefits of decentralized governance are not concentrated but distributed across the community.

Socially, ethical governance encompasses fostering a culture of respect, inclusion, and accountability. The call is for community members to actively contribute to the creation of positive and supportive environments within DAOs. The challenge is to address issues of harassment, discrimination, and power imbalances, creating governance models that are not only effective but also ethical in their treatment of individuals.

Regulatorily, ethical governance involves engaging with regulatory bodies to establish frameworks that encourage responsible innovation. DAOs are called to actively contribute to discussions on ethical considerations, data privacy, and user protection. The challenge is to proactively address concerns raised by regulators, demonstrating a commitment to ethical conduct and a willingness to collaborate in creating a regulatory framework that aligns with decentralized principles.

A Dynamic Call: Navigating the Uncharted Territories

The call to action is not a static decree but a dynamic summons that evolves with the ever-changing landscape of decentralized governance. As we navigate uncharted territories, the call resounds with a spirit of exploration, experimentation, and collective endeavor. ICP DAOs, as vanguards in this journey, are at the forefront of shaping the future of decentralized governance, and the call is for all stakeholders to actively participate in this ongoing narrative.

Technologically, the dynamic call involves exploring new frontiers of blockchain innovation. This includes advancements in consensus mechanisms, the integration of emerging technologies like AI and IoT, and the continual refinement of smart contract functionalities. The challenge is to embrace a mindset of exploration, recognizing that the decentralized landscape is continually evolving, and there is always more to discover.

Economically, the dynamic call challenges stakeholders to experiment with novel economic models.

This involves the exploration of governance tokenomics, the creation of sustainable incentive structures, and the development of mechanisms that foster economic inclusivity. The challenge is to move beyond established paradigms, adapt to changing economic landscapes, and explore innovative approaches to value distribution.

Socially, the dynamic call is an invitation to actively shape the culture and dynamics of decentralized communities. This involves experimentation with governance mechanisms that enhance community participation, the creation of inclusive spaces, and the exploration of new forms of digital collaboration. The challenge is to recognize that social dynamics within DAOs are fluid and subject to change, requiring continual adaptation and innovation.

Regulatorily, the dynamic call challenges regulators and decentralized entities to engage in an ongoing dialogue. This involves a commitment to understanding the unique challenges and opportunities presented by decentralized governance. The challenge is to move away from static regulatory frameworks and embrace a dynamic approach that evolves in response to the rapidly changing landscape of blockchain technologies.

A Collective Symphony: Orchestrating the Future of Decentralized Governance

In answering this dynamic call to action, a collective symphony emerges—a harmonious collaboration of developers, community members, regulators, and innovators orchestrating the future of decentralized governance. Each stakeholder plays a unique instrument in this symphony, contributing their skills, insights, and passion to create a composition that transcends individual contributions.

Developers, with their technical prowess, are instrumental in crafting the melodies of innovation. The call is for a symphony that resonates with the brilliance of cutting-edge technologies, secure and scalable infrastructures, and interoperable frameworks. The challenge is to harmonize the diverse elements of blockchain development, creating a melody that propels decentralized governance into new heights of possibility.

Community members, as active participants in this symphony, bring the richness of their diverse perspectives and experiences. The call is for a symphony that echoes with inclusivity, transparency, and meaningful participation. The challenge is to create a vibrant and dynamic community culture, where every voice is heard, and every participant feels a sense of belonging in the collective creation of decentralized governance.

Regulators, as key conductors in this symphony, shape the regulatory frameworks that harmonize with the melodies of innovation. The call is for a symphony that strikes a balance between fostering innovation and safeguarding against potential risks. The challenge is to conduct with an ear to the nuances of decentralized technologies, ensuring that regulations contribute to the crescendo of responsible and ethical decentralized governance.

Innovators, with their spirit of exploration and experimentation, compose the symphony's avant-garde elements. The call is for a symphony that pushes boundaries, challenges norms, and embraces the unknown. The challenge is to explore uncharted territories, experiment with novel governance models, and contribute to the continual evolution of decentralized ecosystems.

As this collective symphony unfolds, it becomes a testament to the transformative potential of ICP DAOs and the broader decentralized governance movement. It is a symphony that transcends individual contributions, creating a harmonious narrative of empowerment, inclusivity, and innovation. The dynamic call to action becomes the guiding score, leading the way to a future where decentralized governance is not just a technological innovation but a symphony of collective empowerment and collaboration.

THE END

Glossary

Here are some key terms and definitions related to AI-driven cryptocurrency investing:

1. DAO (Decentralized Autonomous Organization): A DAO is an organization represented by rules encoded as a computer program that is transparent, controlled by the organization members, and not influenced by a central government.

2. ICP (Internet Computer Protocol): ICP refers to a protocol enabling the operation of the Internet Computer, a blockchain-based network that aims to extend the functionality of the internet into a decentralized and secure environment.

3. Decentralized Governance: Decentralized governance involves distributing decision-making authority across a network, often facilitated by blockchain technology, reducing reliance on centralized authorities.

4. Network Nervous System (NNS): NNS is a crucial component of the Internet Computer Protocol, functioning as the governance mechanism that oversees network upgrades, canister economics, and network security.

5. Canister Smart Contracts: Canisters are smart contracts on the Internet Computer, encapsulating code and

data, enabling decentralized applications to function without reliance on a central server.

6. Chain-key Cryptography: Chain-key cryptography is a method used in the ICP DAO system to secure the foundational elements of the network, ensuring cryptographic integrity and privacy.

7. Asynchronous Byzantine Fault Tolerance (aBFT): aBFT is a consensus algorithm employed by ICP DAOs to ensure network resilience by tolerating and recovering from Byzantine faults, even in asynchronous network conditions.

8. Subnets: Subnets in the ICP DAO ecosystem are partitions of the network that enable scalability and diversity, allowing for specialized functionalities and governance structures.

9. Governance Tokenomics: Governance tokenomics refers to the economic models governing the distribution and use of tokens within a DAO, aligning incentives and encouraging active participation in governance processes.

10. Proposal Creation and Voting Process: This involves the initiation and approval process within a DAO, where community members propose changes or decisions, and the community votes to determine their acceptance.

11. DAO Evolution and Adaptation: The capacity of a DAO to evolve and adapt to changing circumstances,

technologies, and community needs, ensuring its continued relevance and effectiveness.

12. Securing ICP DAOs: The process of implementing measures to protect assets, data, and the overall integrity of ICP DAOs, enhancing trust and mitigating potential risks.

13. Community-Driven Governance: A governance model where decisions within a DAO are determined by active participation and input from its community members.

14. Decentralized Finance (DeFi): DeFi refers to financial services built on blockchain and decentralized technologies, often involving smart contracts and governance by DAOs.

15. Social Impact and Community Initiatives: Involves the application of ICP DAOs to drive positive change in society, supporting non-profit organizations, community projects, and social impact initiatives.

16. Interoperability: The capability of ICP DAOs to interact and integrate with other blockchain networks, fostering collaboration and the seamless flow of assets and information.

17. Legal Landscape for ICP DAOs: The regulatory framework governing the operation of ICP DAOs, including compliance requirements and legal considerations.

18. Intellectual Property Rights (IPR) and ICP DAOs: Involves the legal considerations related to the protection of intellectual property within the ICP DAO ecosystem, safeguarding innovation and creativity.

19. Taxation and Financial Compliance: Navigating the tax implications and ensuring financial compliance within the ICP DAO environment, addressing fiscal responsibilities.

20. Data Privacy and Security in ICP DAOs: Measures and protocols implemented to protect user data and ensure privacy within the ICP DAO ecosystem.

21. Designing and Implementing an ICP DAO: The step-by-step process of conceptualizing, creating, and launching an ICP DAO, involving both technical and governance considerations.

22. Community Engagement and Stakeholder Participation Strategies: The methodologies employed to actively involve community members and stakeholders in the decision-making processes of ICP DAOs.

23. Managing Risk and Mitigating Challenges in ICP DAOs: Strategies for identifying, assessing, and addressing potential risks and challenges to ensure the robustness and resilience of ICP DAOs.

24. Measuring Success and Assessing Impact in ICP DAOs: The evaluation of key performance indicators and qualitative factors to gauge the effectiveness and impact of ICP DAOs.

25. Recapping the Transformative Potential of ICP DAOs: Summarizing the revolutionary capabilities and implications of ICP DAOs in reshaping governance structures.

26. Addressing Future Challenges and Opportunities: Anticipating and strategizing for the challenges and opportunities that lie ahead in the evolution of ICP DAOs.

27. A Call to Action: Embracing the Future of Decentralized Governance with ICP DAOs: An appeal for active participation and commitment from stakeholders to contribute to the widespread adoption and success of ICP DAOs.

Potential References

Introduction:

Buterin, V., & Poon, J. (2014). "A Next-Generation Smart Contract and Decentralized Application Platform." Ethereum White Paper. Retrieved from https://ethereum.org/en/whitepaper/

Williams, T. (2021). "Internet Computer: A Blockchain Computer for the Internet." DFINITY Foundation. Retrieved from https://dfinity.org/

Larimer, D. (2013). "Delegated Proof-of-Stake Consensus." BitShares Wiki. Retrieved from https://docs.bitshares.org/bitshares/dpos.html

Chapter 1: The Technological Foundation of ICP DAOs:

Narayanan, A., Bonneau, J., Felten, E., Miller, A., & Goldfeder, S. (2016). "Bitcoin and Cryptocurrency Technologies: A Comprehensive Introduction." Princeton University Press.

Micali, S. (2018). "Algorand: The Efficient and Democratic Ledger." Algorand. Retrieved from https://www.algorand.com/resources/papers/general

DFINITY. (2022). "Internet Computer: Network Nervous System (NNS)." Retrieved from https://sdk.dfinity.org/docs/network-nervous-system/index.html

Chapter 2: The Mechanics of ICP DAOs:

Vitalik Buterin. (2018). "Ethereum: A Next-Generation Smart Contract and Decentralized Application Platform." Retrieved from https://ethereum.org/en/whitepaper/

Hoskinson, C. (2021). "Cardano: A Blockchain Platform for the Change-makers of the World." Cardano Foundation. Retrieved from https://cardano.org/

Chapter 3: ICP DAOs in Action: Empowering Real-World Applications:

Casey, M. J., & Vigna, P. (2018). "The Truth Machine: The Blockchain and the Future of Everything." St. Martin's Press.

Tapscott, D., & Tapscott, A. (2016). "Blockchain Revolution: How the Technology Behind Bitcoin and Other Cryptocurrencies is Changing the World." Penguin.

Chapter 4: The Future of ICP DAOs: A Vision for Decentralized Governance:

Swan, M. (2015). "Blockchain: Blueprint for a New Economy." O'Reilly Media.

Antonopoulos, A. M. (2017). "Mastering Bitcoin: Unlocking Digital Cryptocurrencies." O'Reilly Media.

Chapter 5: Legal and Regulatory Considerations for ICP DAOs:

Zohar, A. (2015). "Bitcoin: under the Hood." Communications of the ACM, 58(9), 104–113.

Casey, M. J., & Vigna, P. (2018). "The Truth Machine: The Blockchain and the Future of Everything." St. Martin's Press.

Chapter 6: Realizing the Potential of ICP DAOs: A Practical Guide for Implementation:

Mougayar, W. (2016). "The Business Blockchain: Promise, Practice, and Application of the Next Internet Technology." John Wiley & Sons.

Wood, G. (2014). "Ethereum: A Secure Decentralized Generalized Transaction Ledger." Ethereum Project Yellow Paper. Retrieved from https://ethereum.github.io/yellowpaper/paper.pdf

Conclusion:

Tapscott, D., & Tapscott, A. (2016). "Blockchain Revolution: How the Technology Behind Bitcoin and Other Cryptocurrencies is Changing the World." Penguin.

Narayanan, A., Bonneau, J., Felten, E., Miller, A., & Goldfeder, S. (2016). "Bitcoin and Cryptocurrency Technologies: A Comprehensive Introduction." Princeton University Press.

www.ingramcontent.com/pod-product-compliance
Lightning Source LLC
LaVergne TN
LVHW012039070526
838202LV00056B/5544